WHY
WORKERS
QUIT

and Other Powerful Insights From The Largest
Workforce Survey Ever Conducted on the
Restoration Industry

THE KNOWHOW TEAM

Dedicated to the restoration workers of
yesterday, today, and tomorrow

> **"**
>
> # EMPLOYEES DON'T QUIT JOBS, THEY QUIT MANAGERS.
>
> \- Steve Miranda, Managing Director at Cornell University
>
> **"**

Table of Contents

1

The Great Resignation, and the Restoration Industry's Path Forward

CHAPTER 1

Introduction

The Great Resignation, and the Restoration
Industry's Path Forward

L eaders in the restoration industry today face a unique dilemma. The rising frequency of catastrophic events coupled with aging infrastructure has created more project opportunities than ever before, while at the very same time, attracting and retaining today's worker has never been more challenging.

Talented, disciplined restorers are a unique breed, and they know it.

In response to all this, companies today find themselves in one of two camps: those that are currently experiencing significant workforce challenges, and those that are about to. The data points clearly to one clear overarching reality:

Restoration companies that fail to adapt to the needs and wants of the new labor worker will not be here in the next five years.

As the COVID-19 pandemic swept North America in the Spring of 2020, every political pundit had their opinion on its long-term impact on the economy and how it would make life harder for business owners.

Many of them were right, and restoration businesses in particular went through hell and back. From changing health restrictions to work-from-home orders and a supply chain nightmare, running a restoration company during the pandemic tested the resolve and ability of even the most experienced leadership teams.

The narrative many of us told ourselves is that one day we would emerge from the chaos and things will go back to normal. Now two years later, we have all come to realize that 'normal' is not coming back.

Instead, restoration leaders are being hit with arguably an even greater crisis than an invisible virus: an epidemic of growing worker discontent and frustration, leading to the biggest mass employee resignation in the history of the United States. Dubbed The Great Resignation, this new era of worker pushback

Resignations per month in the United States

Source: U.S. Bureau of Labor Statistics, Job Openings and Labor Turnover Survey

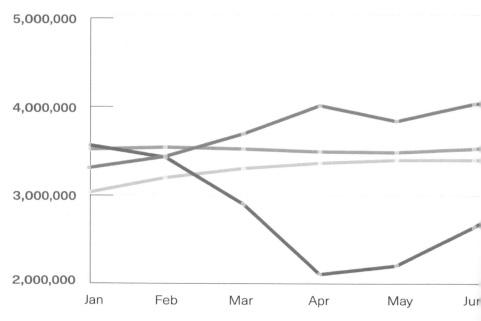

is wreaking more havoc on an already battered and fragmented restoration industry.

Leaders have been pushed to their wits' end.

For owners and managers in the restoration industry, The Great Resignation isn't just a headline on a late-night cable news show - it's their reality.

This book documents the chasm that is growing between managers and workers in the restoration industry, from the mouth of the restorers themselves. With first-of-its-kind data from the largest survey ever conducted on the restoration workforce, it highlights where workers feel they're being failed, and the path to growth and success amidst The Great Resignation.

Managers and leaders across the United States are throwing their hands up in frustration, unaware as to why their workers are turning on them and walking out the door.

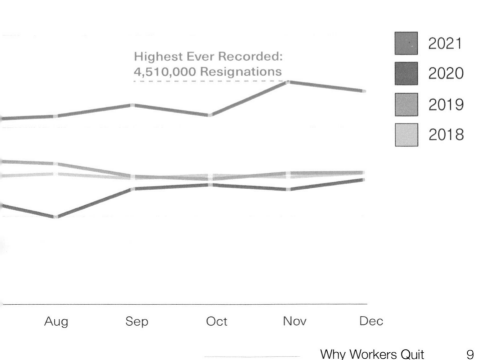

The situation is high stakes, but according to our research, there is a specific navigable path forward - however, you must act now.

The answers to combating The Great Resignation are out there, and this book gives you a direct line to the source of this unrest, and a way out of it: your workers.

The Great Resignation

The autopsy on all the factors that led to the biggest mass exodus of workers in the United States is still ongoing, but the facts don't lie, and they don't care about our feelings. An unprecedented number of employees are walking away from their jobs, trading in their aprons, hard hats, and keyboards for the allure of something better.

How many employees are we talking about here? According to the United States Department of Labor, 4.5 million workers quit their jobs in November 2021 (roughly 3% of the entire workforce).

This is the biggest mass resignation ever reported in the history of the United States - it's a big deal.

Today's restoration leader feels like they're being pressured from all angles. But it doesn't have to be that way.

Scan to tweet!

No one can bury their head in the sand and ignore this, as the consequences of the Great Resignation are not confined to a single workplace. Anyone who has tried to purchase anything in the past year can confirm: wait times are longer, supply chains are stretched, prices for consumer goods are going through the roof, and even ordering a burger at Wendy's can be a chaotic experience if they don't have enough staff.

Leaders in every industry have had no time to step back and assess what is causing the bleeding or how to get it to stop - they are too

Restorers often meet customers on the worst day of their lives

busy trying to keep the lights on and prevent their business from becoming the Great Resignation's next victim. And as bad as this staffing challenge is in industries across the United States, it threatens to be the straw that breaks the camel's back in the restoration industry. Much like looking at a delicious display of baked treats through a locked glass door, restorers see a surplus of project opportunities all around them, but lack sufficient staff to respond - a cruel reality after two years of frazzled operations.

The Perfect Storm

For the past decade, any leader or manager in the restoration in- dustry would have told you the number one thing keeping them up at night is figuring out how to attract and retain high-quality workers. Restoration, like most labor intensive industries, suffers from high-turnover, with many companies struggling to keep their best staff from year-to-year. Combine that with the high level of expertise and industry knowledge required to tackle the broad variety of projects that pop up on any given day, and you've got a recipe for chronically under-trained staff that leave the job site feeling frustrated, under supported and mentally fatigued. With workforces running at threadbare levels, proper onboarding, training, and support is often a luxury that exhausted managers fail to deliver, adding to this vicious cycle.

Yet this is only the tip of the iceberg of why it is so difficult for restorers to keep their best employees around (and recruit new ones). Inflexible pricing from insurance carriers means wages for any specific role have a very limited ceiling, and the fact that restorers are often meeting people on the worst days of their lives means they're not always welcomed with open arms and a basket of brownies. Instead, they can feel like they're being pressured from all angles - the insurance carrier, the customer, the adjustor, and with the minimal margin for error and fatigue levels high, their co-workers themselves.

Managers that don't know what workers want guarantee a revolving door of talent for years to come.

Scan to tweet!

These were the conditions in the restoration industry *prior* to the biggest voluntary worker exodus the United States has ever seen.

To state the obvious, things have only gotten worse.

As a result, many restoration companies are struggling to keep their head above water, and managers and leaders are hanging on by a thread. An industry that already fights tooth and nail to find workers that will reliably meet expectations is swept up in a nationwide storm of worker apathy and frustration, and without a life raft, many businesses risk going under.

When the whole room is spinning, it's difficult to focus clearly on what is right in front of you. For managers and leaders in the restoration industry, today's workforce challenges can only be resolved in one way: by understanding the unique needs and demands of today's workforce.

Today's Worker

It's no secret that Millennial and Gen Z workers have a different make-up than their predecessors.

Whereas prior generations of workers could be motivated by a steady paycheck or fancy perks, these tactics aren't the prime motivators of today's workforce. In fact, it's common to hear stories of employees giving up guaranteed income to pursue something more important to them - a decision that would have been considered very counter-cultural only ten years ago.

What gets these employees out of bed has proven mysterious, and the mass exodus of millions of them across the United States in the wake of the COVID-19 pandemic, when so many others were praying and hoping for job security, only adds to the confusion. But the future of the restoration industry hinges on leaders getting the right answers to these questions, and knowing where to find them.

Any manager that doesn't know what it is these workers want is guaranteeing a revolving door for years to come; rolling the dice every time a talented employee walks in, not knowing if they'll stick around, why they stayed, or why their workers quit.

As Jack Welch, the famous and notorious Chief Executive Officer of General Electric described in his book *Winning*, he had a regular practice of hosting town-hall meetings with his full staff. Any worker who wanted to have their voice heard could grab

Facts at a Glance

450+	50	4,924
The number of respondents to the Restoration Workforce Survey across North America	The number of open-ended questions asked about every aspect of working in the restoration industry	The number of valuable responses received on every aspect of life in the restoration industry

the microphone and share their perspective. After providing a particularly insightful recommendation, one worker commented "for 30 years you've paid me for my hands, when you could have had my brain for free!"

For decades, managers have held meetings providing educated guesses on how to bring new workers into the industry, but this has only led to the stark management-worker divide that exists today. For all the ideas thrown at the wall, there has never been an industry-wide effort to give the workers themselves the microphone and let them tell us exactly what it is they're looking for.

Until now.

The Restoration Workforce Survey

KnowHow is a mobile-first software platform that helps restoration companies become process-driven organizations and

Respondents to the Restoration Workforce Survey
Grouped by age and gender

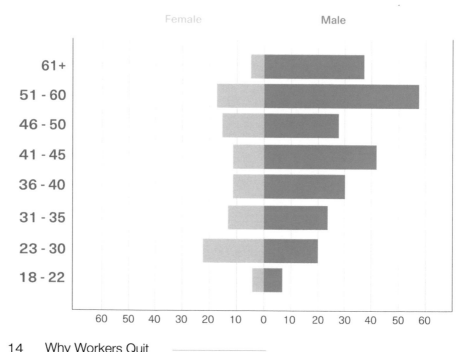

adapt to the needs of the new labor worker. With KnowHow, companies are able to standardize operations in every department and provide their workforces with a single source of truth for all company how-to, in any worker language.

At KnowHow, we believe that the heart of the restoration industry is the labor worker - they are the ones that determine whether the customer leaves a positive review or a scathing one, and they are the ones that can mean the difference between profitability and loss. When workers have the information they need to do their jobs well, they feel empowered, work harder, are more efficient, and contribute positively to team culture. When they feel out-of-the-loop, undertrained, or overly reliant on supervisor input to do a good job, they feel frustrated, produce poor quality work, and begin browsing online job boards on their lunch break.

For too long, the needs of the emerging labor worker have been neglected, and the health of the entire industry is starting to show cracks as a result. In response, KnowHow teamed up with many of the biggest names in the restoration industry, including:

- C&R Magazine
- Business Mentors
- Violand Management Associates
- AiME
- The Restoration Lawyer
- Gearhart and Associates, LLC.
- Restoration & Remediation Magazine
- CORE Group
- Blue Collar Nation
- Restoration Technical Institute

The worker is the heart of the restoration company

The result was the largest survey ever conducted on the restoration industry workforce, dubbed the Restoration Workforce Survey. For the first time ever, hundreds of restoration workers, in the middle of The Great Resignation, were asked detailed questions about their work experience. What was your motivation for joining your company? What was your onboarding experience like? What are the most and least fulfilling parts of your job? Why do good people quit your company? And a host of nearly thirty other targeted questions were posed to hundreds of workers.

The survey provided a candid, unfiltered, and extensive deep dive into the changing landscape of the modern labor worker.

Crucially, the survey was completely anonymous, and the questions were open-ended. We had no intention of being told what we wanted to hear, we only wanted the raw, honest truth. In order to cultivate a compelling work environment that will attract the next generation of worker to the restoration industry, we needed to properly see the industry from the workers' perspective.

A Clear Roadmap

Though workers responding to the Restoration Workforce Survey were free to answer our questions however they'd like, very clear patterns emerged. When we segmented responses into different cohorts by age, job function, gender and more, we saw an even starker contrast between the "old way" of doing things and the future of work. The result of the Restoration Workforce Survey was a detailed breakdown into the way new employees think, what they look for in a workplace, their ideal relationship with their manager, and dozens of other critical insights that could make the difference between success and failure in your company.

Once we processed these insights, we collaborated with seasoned leaders in the restoration industry to make sense of it all, and how this newfound knowledge impacts the average restoration company.

The final product is this book, an authoritative guidebook for restoration industry leaders and managers looking to win with the emerging workforce, and in turn grow and scale their company over the next decade. What you have in your hands is a data-fueled, fact-driven, comprehensive manual that will give you key critical insights into the perspective of every employee in your organization and ensure your company is still around in ten years.

By the end of this book, you'll have a clear, tangible guide to:
- Positioning your company to attract the next generation of workers
- Giving new employees an incredible onboarding experience
- Optimizing employees' relationship with their manager
- Doubling-down on the unique aspects of the job each worker enjoys the most
- Keeping your best workers around for longer, and turning them into champions for your company

What you won't find in this book are vague management philosophies from business school graduates or advice from people afraid to get their hands dirty. This book is filled with the words of workers themselves, telling you exactly what they need from you for your restoration company to be a place they would be eager to work at and tell their friends about. This is a data-driven manual of insights and tactics to give you the greatest possible advantage in attracting and retaining the talent that is going to go the extra mile with your customer, keep your margins high and build an award-winning team culture.

Harness the Future, Don't Fight It

The restoration industry is at an inflection point. The balance of power across the United States has shifted to the worker, and each leader has a critical choice to make.

Those that listen to workers and adapt will emerge from the Great Resignation stronger than they were before the pandemic.

They'll find themselves in a workplace that naturally attracts the high quality staff they've been looking for, with a roster of A-players across every level and each department of the organization.

Those that dig their heels in and refuse to change will see the few bright spots in their organization eventually fade, and take the company's best days with them.

You've got the ability to breathe life into your organization by heeding the words of workers in the restoration industry when they've got the microphone.

What follows is what they had to say. Will you listen?

Want a free digital copy of *Why Workers Quit*?

Scan this QR code and we will e-mail you a free copy of this book, as well as some bonus resources, as our way of saying thanks!

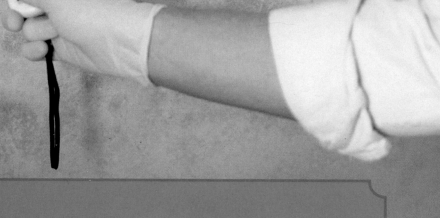

2

Why and How Restoration Workers Switch Jobs

CHAPTER 2

Why Should I Work For You?

Why and How Restoration Workers Switch Jobs

E very job starts with a job offer, but even before that, workers have to decide they want to work for you. In a crowded river with bait everywhere, why did your employees choose you? How did they even end up in the restoration industry?

Simply put, if you don't know where your employees came from or where your next hires will come from, you'll have no idea where to look. Restorers that win among today's workforce deeply understand their staff's career goals and why they wake up in the morning. This means having a clear picture of why they got into restoration, what they were doing beforehand, and what motivated them to land at their current destination.

Was the average young restorer roped into the business by their family? Was it nothing more than a random job posting, at the right place at the right time? Do they simply swim to the biggest salary?

You're reading this because you want to find more high-quality workers, and we want to connect you to the mouth of the river. If there is a pool of latent restorers ready to be activated, we wanted to be the first to know, so the Restoration Workforce Survey did a deep dive on where your workers came from, what industry they worked in previously, and what motivated them to choose to work for you, instead of your competitor.

The results have drastic implications for recruiting, training, and employee retention. Chances are you don't want sloppy seconds, you want to know where to find the best employees, and how you can motivate them.

The responses we received affirmed some current assumptions in the restoration industry, but also provided a fascinating glimpse into untapped markets for new staff, and how you can win them over beyond simply throwing money at them.

If you're sick of returning home with your nets empty, we've got good news: the fish are out there, and they're hungry. Here's how to find them:

Where Are They Coming From?

If we were to ask you what your next star employee is doing right now, what would you answer?

Seriously, take a second to pause and think about this: where is your next high-quality worker today? What are they doing right now?

📈 **Facts at a Glance: Chapter 2**

48%
of survey respondents had no construction experience before their current restoration job

24%
of millennials chose their current role because of the company's strong team culture or leadership

45%
of restoration workers found their current job via a referral by friends or family

---

Where Did You Work Prior to your Current Role?

Responses from the 2022 Restoration Workforce Survey

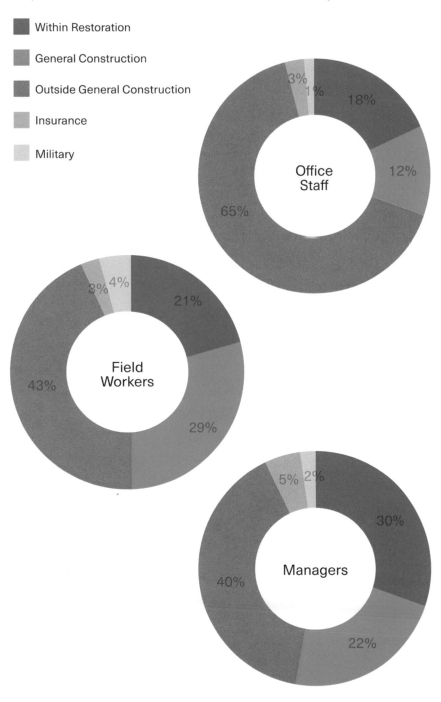

Within Restoration

General Construction

Outside General Construction

Insurance

Military

Office Staff
3%
1%
18%
12%
65%

Field Workers
3% 4%
21%
43%
29%

Managers
5% 2%
30%
40%
22%

If you're like most managers in the restoration industry, you'd assume they're working for a different restoration company. In this view, the best workers jump around from company to company, and every business is constantly under threat of having their employees poached by the new guy in town with more money in his pocket. If this was the case, managers would have every right to be paranoid that their best employees could walk out the door at any moment, and they'd have no way to recruit new, high-quality staff unless they were willing to pay even more than their competitors.

Thankfully, according to the Restoration Workforce Survey, this isn't true.

Roughly 48% of the hundreds of workers surveyed came into the restoration industry from outside general construction, meaning they have no hands-on construction experience at all. They certainly weren't poached from a competitor.

You're limiting your pool of candidates if you only hire experienced restorers

With such a high percentage coming from outside restoration, this means that employers have a rare opportunity here for a fresh start; a clean slate. This is 48% of the workforce walking into their first restoration job without bad habits or preconceived ideas about how work should be done that you need to undo. These are green workers who you can form into doing things the way you believe they should be; a fresh pot of clay.

Hiring workers new to the restoration industry gives companies a clean slate and an opportunity to define the right way to do things.

Scan to tweet!

As we'll dive deep into in Chapter 3, our data reveals the new labor worker desires a high-level of structure in their onboarding, training and support. Whereas many managers view a worker's first two weeks as a proverbial 'trial by fire', workers today view their first two weeks as an extended assessment of their new employer's company. If the first two weeks were unstructured and chaotic, the worker assumes this is a foreshadowing of what the next two months and two years would be like, and they quickly exit stage left with little notice given in search of their next opportunity.

> 66
> **I'm always trying to learn new skills. I discovered an opportunity in restoration while I was looking for a new job.**
> - Millennial Project Manager, 99 Oregon

Today's worker is not flaky, they deeply desire to lay down roots and join a team.

But they are picky, and use their first weeks on the job to get a lay of the land before settling in for the long haul.

Of course, this then puts the responsibility on you, the manager, to provide proper training. But this is far from a negative - instead, this could be your company's greatest advantage.

Never before has there been a greater competitive advantage for companies that become process-driven organizations. Process-driven restoration companies attract and retain top talent by delivering a structured, intentional experience from day one. They have the ability to take any motivated worker, regardless of their experience level, and turn them into efficient, productive extensions of the company's 'way' of doing things.

> 66
> **I previously worked in a bakery, and joined the restoration industry because I wanted a new direction in life.**
> - Millennial Office Administrator, Pennsylvania 99

How do these companies become process-driven? By building standardized, repeatable processes that can be put in the hands of any employee in any role, and equip them with the on-demand guidance to succeed. This company-wide way of doing things can be systematically taught to new recruits, whether they've been in the industry for 20 years or 20 minutes. Considering the majority of your new hires will fall into the latter category, this "crash course in restoration" will give them the expertise they need to do things the right way. For those with more experience, a standardized process becomes an opportunity to weed out any old, unreliable methods they have in the back of their mind and start implementing data-driven operations for success.

> 66
> **The culture seemed amazing, the work was challenging, and I could tell there would be something new to learn every day.**
> - Millennial Office Administrator, Pennsylvania 99

Take a step back and imagine the impact a tightly-defined road-map for onboarding employees would have in your company.

While your competitors would be forced to rely on the usual channels, you could take any motivated worker, from any background, and put in their hands the keys to success in their role. With the work they need to do clearly defined, they would be doing their job the right way from Day 1, with little need for costly training programs, or constant manager interruption.

Most importantly, you would have an unfair advantage in recruiting, as your prospect pool would be 10x larger than every other restoration company in town.

The restoration companies that win with this new generation of workers are the ones that have the ability to recruit from any industry and turn their employees into productive powerhouses through standardized, repeatable processes for every role.

Becoming a Stickier Workplace

Moving on from the 48% of workers who come to the restoration industry from outside of general construction, the next largest source of new workers, unsurprisingly, come from within the restoration industry. Barely making up 28% of new hires, this group is significantly smaller than those from outside general construction.

> 66
>
> **Previously I worked for a competitor, but I switched to my current job because it was a better opportunity.**
>
> - Millennial Manager, 99
>   Arizona

What this means is that employers' fears are somewhat founded; other companies to an extent can steal from your pool of workers, especially if those workers are already seeking greener pastures. Though a certain percentage of workers will shop around, as the data reveals in later chapters, the majority of the turnover in restoration businesses is due to a company's own leaky bucket. This means that the onus is on leaders to fix that leak, before the 28% of the workforce that keeps its eyes out for new opportunities within industry exits their own company stage right.

If you're a restoration leader, how can you make sure your employees stick around, even if they are offered more money elsewhere? As we'll soon see, a lot of factors go into an employee's decision to work for you versus your competitor, and money is only a small part of the equation. Companies that know what their workers are looking for in a job have the ability to tailor their role to meet those needs, providing them with a valuable buffer against higher salaries elsewhere.

Finally, there is a small, but significant pool of workers coming from the insurance sector (4%) and the military (2.5%). These numbers are important because they demonstrate potential for

What are the Reasons You Accepted Your Current Role?

Responses from the 2022 Restoration Workforce Survey - Grouped by Role

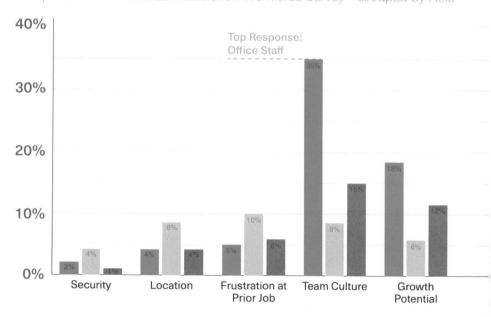

future growth. There are specific industries out there that have an appetite for restoration. What does this mean for you? Do you have a veteran employee? If not, know that your competition probably does. You can take advantage of this data by leaving job postings at a nearby base or the local Veterans Association.

Why They Took the Job

When Restoration Workforce Survey respondents were asked why they chose to work for their current company, the top two answers were firstly, the strong team culture, and secondly, the opportunity for career or skill growth.

However, dive a little deeper and the results get even more fascinating below the surface.

When we segmented these responses by role, we discovered a massive, unignorable disparity in responses depending on the type of work done.

Among office staff, the allure of a sticky team culture was 204% stronger than it was to their colleagues in the field or in management. As one worker put it, "the work here aligned with my

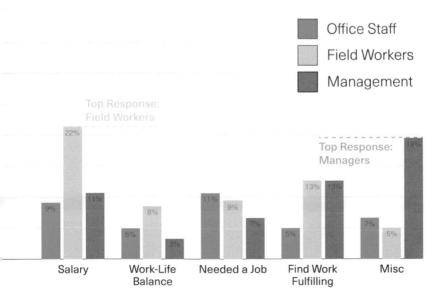

degree, it's something that I'm passionate about, and the culture in this company is better than my previous one. I enjoy being treated with respect and equality."

Office staff have hundreds of micro-interactions with co-workers on any given day, so companies that can boast a strong team-first culture will have an inherent advantage in recruiting these workers.

Likewise, office workers were motivated by the opportunity for career growth more than field technicians or management. Many survey responses pointed to their current role being the next step in their career, or it being a challenging upgrade from what they were doing previously. Because very few employees in this group mentioned they found their work inherently fulfilling, the onus is on managers and recruiters to help them clearly see how the work they're doing today will take them to where they want to go in the future, call it 'Career Context'. Restoration leaders that successfully do this will be able to lure talented office staff from other industries, and competitors, and help them find the career momentum they may feel like they're lacking elsewhere.

> 66
> **I could tell this company had strong family values. When I asked around, they had a good reputation.**
>
> - Gen X Office Administrator, Washington 99

Why Field Technicians Want to Work For You

All of this stands in contrast to the frontline technician, who are motivated by a very different set of factors.

Only 8% of field workers chose their current job because they felt attracted to its team culture, which makes sense considering the more solitary environment out on the jobsite. Instead, a variety of influences guided the field technician's decision to accept

What are the Reasons You Accepted Your Current Role?

Responses from the 2022 Restoration Workforce Survey - Grouped by Age

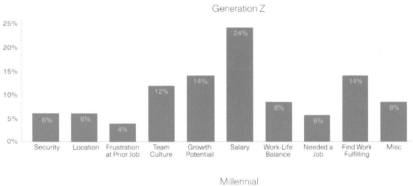

Generation Z

Security	6%
Location	6%
Frustration at Prior Job	4%
Team Culture	12%
Growth Potential	14%
Salary	24%
Work-Life Balance	8%
Needed a Job	6%
Find Work Fulfilling	14%
Misc	8%

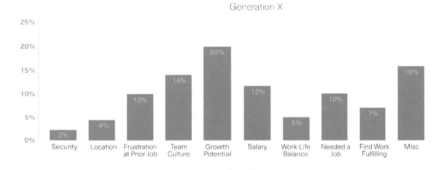

Millennial

Security	—
Location	1%
Frustration at Prior Job	6%
Team Culture	24%
Growth Potential	23%
Salary	13%
Work-Life Balance	3%
Needed a Job	6%
Find Work Fulfilling	19%
Misc	5%

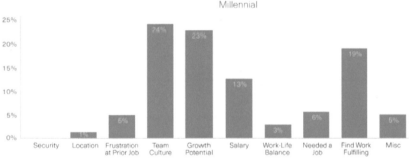

Generation X

Security	2%
Location	4%
Frustration at Prior Job	10%
Team Culture	14%
Growth Potential	20%
Salary	12%
Work-Life Balance	5%
Needed a Job	10%
Find Work Fulfilling	7%
Misc	16%

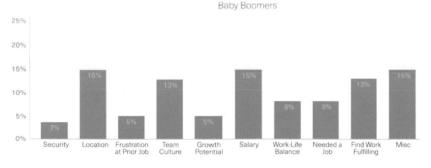

Baby Boomers

Security	3%
Location	15%
Frustration at Prior Job	5%
Team Culture	13%
Growth Potential	5%
Salary	15%
Work-Life Balance	8%
Needed a Job	8%
Find Work Fulfilling	13%
Misc	15%

their current role, including finding the work of restoring people's homes inherently fulfilling, and frustration with their previous job or supervisor.

However, there's one clear reason field technicians will choose a certain restoration company over its competitor, and it was the answer every owner was hoping to avoid:

Salary.

The data is unapologetic: more than any other role, the frontline worker is more likely to follow the money than his or her co-workers. But we're happy to report that even here there's nuance, and wise leaders in the restoration industry will harness it for their own benefit.

When you segment responses by age, Gen Z is the only age group that is primarily motivated by salary. Millennials care far more about a strong team culture and opportunity for growth than they do salary, and Gen Xers likewise are seeking career advancement more than a big paycheck.

> **In today's workforce, interviewing is as much selling as it is selecting.**
>
> Scan to tweet!

Each of these age groups and roles have their own preferences, and it's only the youngest among the field workers that allow the allure of a big pay day to strongly influence where they end up. This finding is aligned with broader studies on Gen Z workers who, after enduring recessions, global instability, and pandemics, are looking for job stability and some confidence they're going to make ends meet.

But what does this mean for employers?

Companies need to demonstrate to candidates that they have a track record of developing and advancing the careers of their employees

Attracting Quality Candidates

If you are fishing in today's labor pool and only baiting your hook with the promise of salary, then you're only going to attract a certain type of fish. In today's workforce, interviewing is as much selling as it is selecting. Today's candidates know what they want, and if they don't see it in your company, they will take a job with a company more closely aligned with their goals, of which there are many. It's your job as a manager to strengthen your sales pitch to new recruits, or you'll be left in the cold.

For office workers and managers over 25 years old, a strong team culture and rapid growth potential are far more motivating than a higher salary. In order to attract these candidates, you must put

> 66
> **I felt unappreciated at my prior job, and this one offered more money and a greater opportunity for advancement.**
>
> - Millennial Technician, Nova Scotia
> 99

what motivates them on the hook. From job descriptions to your landing page, you must highlight these features.

If a qualified candidate were to ask you, "Tell me about the team culture," how would you respond? Would you simply reference an impromptu BBQ you once organized, or can you give clear, tangible examples of how your company's unique culture shows up in day-to-day work? The company's rituals, values, and unique flavor - pictures help.

45% of workers in the restoration industry discovered their current role through a referral. What does that mean for your recruitment strategy?

Scan to tweet!

Insufficient answers will not cut it with these applicants - and if they don't ask, you might be interviewing a dud. In an era where every organization claims to stand for something, you need to show the impact your company culture has in how work gets done, how employees interact with each other, and the trust management has in their reports (and vice versa).

Would team culture have a greater influence on frontline techs if they were more exposed to it?

Steve Cadigan, contributor to CNBC, Fox News, and author of *Workquake* explains that the best sales pitch when recruiting new hires is simply the truth. "In order for a company to demonstrate they deliver career growth," Steve says, "they need to showcase people who are in the firm (or used to be) that had that great 'growth experience' while there." Can you point to other employees who moved up the ranks in your company, or who are more talented and qualified today than the day they walked into their job? Modern workers want to know you're serious about training and development, so highlight how staff at your company are constantly exposed to new projects, rotated into different departments, and gain new skills.

> 66
>
> **The ability to grow and learn a new industry has always really intrigued me.**
>
> - Gen Z Office Administrator, Texas 99

"Candidates today are looking for career security, not simply job security," Steve explains. "Making them better throughout their tenure with your company is essential." Restoration companies have pictures and case studies highlighting the transformation they are capable of delivering on projects, but few have case studies that show clearly how the company transforms its workers into higher-caliber, more employable people. To stand out, you need to provide these case studies to motivated young applicants.

> 66
>
> **I wanted to provide for my family while also helping out other people currently going through difficult times.**
>
> - Gen X Manager, Michigan 99

Some industry leaders assume that all candidates are only interested in the money, and if they can't afford to pay them more, well then it's game over. The truth is that there's a very small sub-section of workers that are primarily motivated by money, and even that will be insufficient in keeping them around for the long haul. One has to wonder if frontline techs were more exposed to elements of team culture, if it would begin to have a greater influence on whether they stay or go.

As a restoration leader, focus on the elements that are under your control. Can you standardize your hiring and development processes so new hires can see a direct path toward autonomy, more responsibility, raises or promotions? This promotes the growth your company can provide. Can you find new ways to highlight your values in company-wide initiatives or weekly meetings? This promotes team culture.

When candidates come in for interviews, take the time to find out what is motivating them to sit down with you, and make sure you highlight the steps your company is taking to over-deliver on these factors. Show them pictures from your team culture events, or give them the opportunity to meet someone currently working in the role they are applying for who can articulate the company values and vision. Show them a roadmap for the career progress they can experience at your company, including how and when they will be trained.

> 66
> **I saw a company vehicle on the road, called the number, and asked HR if they were hiring. Turns out they were!**
>
> - Millennial Accountant, Maryland
> 99

The Restoration Workforce Survey shows that younger workers are more motivated by finding the work they do inherently fulfilling, so harness this to your benefit. The opportunity for restorers to highlight the company's unique service opportunity to 'restore the lives of homeowners' is one of the most underutilized (and more economical) recruiting incentives. Recruits want to know about the impact their work can have on the lives of others, so show them before and after pictures of the homes your company restored after major natural disasters. Capture short testimonial

Where Did You Discover Your Current Position?
Responses from the 2022 Restoration Workforce Survey

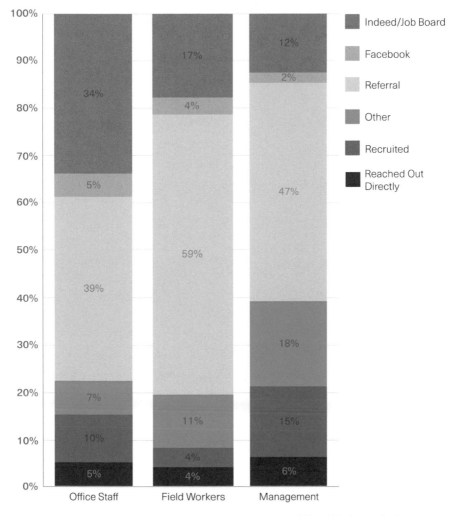

> **66**
>
> **This was a better work environment, better training, better pay, and I could tell they appreciated their employees more.**
>
> - Millennial Estimator, California **99**

clips of emotional clients before and after restoring their homes. Especially for those currently outside the restoration industry considering joining your team, this can help tip the scales and give your company a leg up.

Remember, for the vast majority of workers today, money is not the most important factor.

A strong team culture, clear growth potential, and other elements all heavily influence the decision to join your company vs your competitor.

How They Discovered the Job

So you've adjusted your interviewing 'sales pitch', and you've begun tailoring your interview process to focus on the unique motivators for each candidate. The question then becomes, where will you find them?

> **66**
>
> **I chose this job because there was more potential for growth.**
>
> - Millennial Technician, Washington **99**

According to the Restoration Workforce Survey, your *next* all-star worker is already in the networks of your *current* all-star workers. A staggering amount (45%) of restoration workers found their current job through a friend or family member, and referrals are an especially strong source of field technicians. For employers, this can initially cause concern because

Sifting through resumes is increasingly becoming an outdated strategy. Today, more workers found their current job via a referral from friends and family than any other method.

this method of finding candidates seems largely out of their control. It's not.

Assuming you've cultivated a strong team culture, provide clear growth opportunities, and make your values tangible within your company, creating incentive for your current staff to refer new candidates to the company from their networks only requires a simple strategy. If your current staff enjoys their work environment, then half of the employment battle is already won for you. You can equip your staff to become your sales team, encouraging others to join a successful, unified company.

On the flip side, if your current staff is unhappy, unfulfilled, and unmotivated, then you're missing out on a huge slice of the labor market. No candidate—and especially no younger generation candidate—will want to work for a company that their friend is always complaining about. The truth here is that your team culture can be either a positive feedback loop, or a negative one.

After friends and family, the next most common source of workers was job posting sites like Indeed. To take advantage of this pool of candidates, take another close look at the data: today's workers (particularly office workers, who are more likely to find their next job on Indeed) are interested in team culture and growth potential. Your best bet is to make these clear selling points in your job posting. Yes, the salary should be made available, but more than that, you must convey the sense that you offer a positive work environment and opportunities for career advancement. These factors will pique the interest of quality candidates, as long as your actions match your words. Ensure your job description includes sections like, "Team Culture", "Our Values", and "A Day in the Life at Our Company".

In an era where workers feel like they've been ripped off, and their managers only care about the company's bottom line, you've got the ability to show candidates that you know what they're looking for in a job, and have tailor-made their role to fit those needs.

Combine this with the viral effects of positive workplaces, and you can leverage a great workplace experience to keep your funnel of top candidates constantly full.

Ask any field tech if they've ever been stung by an estimator who over-promised on a job, and you'll likely hear a bunch of expletives before you can finish your question. The unfortunate truth is, despite good intentions, companies are just as susceptible to over-promising and under-delivering when recruiting candidates. Unless their actions match their words, they've built a

> 66
>
> **I saw a clear path to advancement, on-the-job training and improved pay. Most importantly though, I believed in the company mission.**
>
> - Gen X Technician, Maryland
>
> 99

leaky bucket that attracts great workers, but quickly sours them in their first few weeks on the job.

In our next chapter, we'll unpack the fatal mistakes companies make during their first two weeks with a new candidate, and how they can take advantage of this crucial window to set their workers (and themselves) up for success.

☰ Key Takeaways: Chapter 2

- ✓ 48% of workers come from outside restoration or even general construction, offering a clean slate for employers willing to invest in properly training new hires

- ✓ 28% of workers come from within the restoration sector, suggesting that it's an employer's job to be proactive in making their team culture sticky to avoid employees jumping ship

- ✓ Most of today's workers are motivated by factors other than a high salary

- ✓ Even if you can't offer a higher salary, you can notably improve your company's retention by prioritizing team culture and clear career advancement

- ✓ 45% of candidates discovered their job through referrals from friends and family. Employers that have strong culture and growth opportunities can harness the positive experience of their current workers to find more A-players

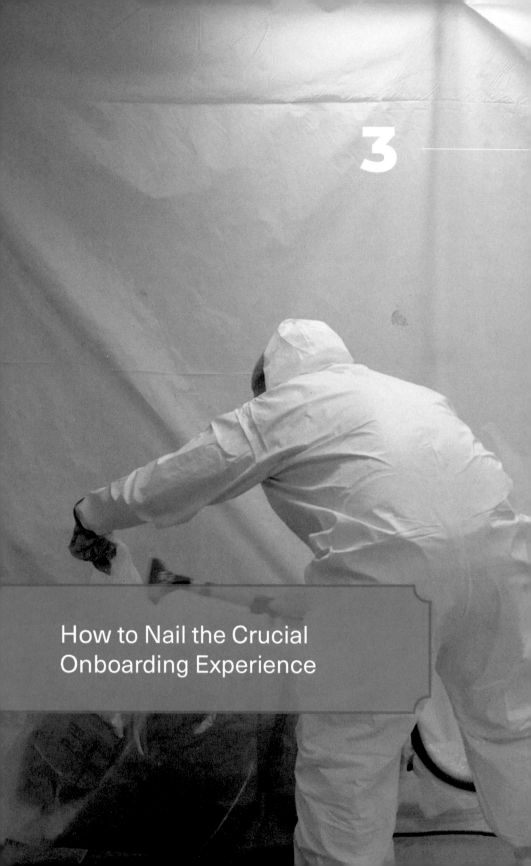

How to Nail the Crucial
Onboarding Experience

CHAPTER 3

First Impressions Matter More than You Think
How to Nail the Crucial Onboarding Experience

There are few periods more important in a worker's tenure at your company than their first two weeks on the job. It's in this critical window that the tone is set for what a worker's relationship is going to be with their manager, how much support they're going to be given, and in light of the previous chapter, whether they believe the promises you made during the interview process about your team culture and growth potential will ever come to fruition.

To put it simply, the seeds planted during a worker's onboarding experience, whether seeds of optimism or seeds of doubt, will take root and influence how they view your company throughout the course of their employment. It's here that companies can either take advantage of a honeymoon period, or give their new employee buyer's remorse.

Unfortunately, many of today's businesses have opted for the latter, letting an unstructured, chaotic first few weeks build a shaky foundation between them and even the best candidates. When new workers see this, they assume this is just how business is done at your company, and start asking themselves if they really want twelve more months of this.

With so much at stake, it's vital that businesses recognize the importance of an intentional roadmap during a worker's first few weeks with the company. Yet the restoration industry finds this particularly difficult for a few reasons:

Restoration is, by nature, a reactive industry. No one schedules a hurricane or flood weeks in advance, so technicians are constantly responding to urgent scenarios, dealing with frantic customers, and often hiring on the fly.

> When the emergency call comes in, too many new hires in the restoration industry are thrown into the thick of it all without proper training.

Scan to tweet!

We've never met a company that didn't have great intentions when it comes to training and equipping new staff, but when the emergency call comes in, new hires are thrown into the thick of it all, expected to learn by shadowing another employee. This leads to many workers being given information "just-in-time", creating a dependency on those around them to fill in their gaps and an entire team of people who must constantly interrupt their managers or co-workers to accomplish their tasks.

Scale this chaotic onboarding experience to an entire organization, and you've got the recipe for manager burn out, unproductive staff, poor quality workmanship, missed carrier expectations

---

📈 **Facts at a Glance: Chapter 3**

75%	**63%**	**13%**
of survey respondents identified opportunities to improve their onboarding experience	of office staff say the best part about their first two weeks is meeting new teammates	less confident are office staff exiting their onboarding training, compared to their peers.

How confident are you that an employee hired in your organization today would be given the tools they need to succeed?

and employees keeping one eye out for a more structured work environment.

So when we say that the restoration industry finds onboarding difficult, what we really mean is that it often doesn't formally onboard employees, period.

Without a standardized training program and a clear explanation of your company's best practices, your employees are playing the telephone game.

An employee that's been with the company for thirty years might explain how to fix a water leak once, but by the time that explanation is conveyed to a new hire, it's been morphed and muddied. With so many fires to put out, management doesn't find out that their employees have been insufficiently trained until they're

> 66
> **I started my job in the middle of Hurricane Ike. It was sink or swim right from Day 1.**
>
> - Gen X Manager, Texas 99

getting call-backs from insurance or complaints from customers of shoddy workmanship.

How confident are you that an employee hired today in your organization would be given the skills they need to succeed in their role? How would they respond to that question? Do you have the courage to ask them?

Would their first two weeks send the impression that they signed onto a company that is intentional, focused, and takes training and skill development seriously? Or would they be thrown into a chaotic environment and left to fend for themselves?

If you're like most restoration leaders, you know that your on-boarding process is not as structured as it should be. But what you might not know is how that's interpreted by today's workforce. So, we surveyed workers about their first few days on the job to find out if this chaos-fueled onboarding process is working for them. According to the data...it's not.

How Effective Was Your Company's Onboarding?

Responses to the 2022 Restoration Workforce Survey

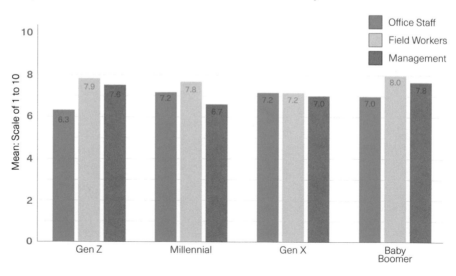

Who Onboarding Is Working For, and Who It's Not

The Restoration Workforce Survey asked employees how effective they felt their onboarding process was, and at face value, everybody seemed relatively satisfied.

However, don't be deceived. There are alarm bells ringing below the surface, and managers ignore them at their own peril.

Younger workers new to the industry, particularly office staff, reported much less confidence coming out of their first two weeks on the job than their peers. To quote one respondent, "I was overwhelmed with information for my role. I was new in the restoration industry, so having all this information dumped on me right away was incredibly stressful. I didn't understand what I was being told and everything was unorganized. It felt like I was expected to know everything and be ready to take a test. It was too much all at once."

This theme is prevalent throughout the responses of Millennial and Gen Z employees new to the industry. The restoration industry is a unique beast, and many workers felt like they were being thrown into the deep end before being taught how to swim.

These environments create negative feedback loops that make it remarkably difficult to properly train and prepare new employees for the road ahead. Unstructured, chaotic onboarding experiences do a poor job equipping workers with the information they

> 66
>
> **My onboarding experience was awful. There was no training, and other techs bullied me because I didn't know anything as a new person. Everyone talked shit about everyone else.**
>
> - Millennial Technician, Texas
>
> 99

need to know to do their jobs successfully. And because the human brain is unable to retain new information well when under duress, the little that *is* taught during these employees' first few weeks often goes in one ear and out the other.

Any restoration leader intent on growing and scaling their business can see the clear problem this creates. For those unsure about where to start, your workers once again have some key insights you won't want to ignore.

Give Me Structure!

Survey respondents were given the opportunity to sound off on what should have gone better during their first two weeks, and over 75% of them agreed that there was room for improvement.

Chief among their complaints was that their training lacked structure and clear guidance. Instead, worker after worker told tales of being thrown into the middle of things, sent out to fight fires before being given the tools to do so. Unclarified role expectations, no background information on the type of work the company does, and general aimlessness over the first two weeks left

What Could Have Been Improved During Your Onboarding?

Responses to the 2022 Restoration Workforce Survey

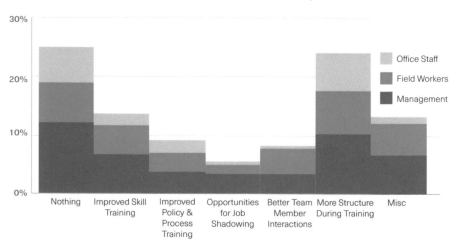

a sour taste in these new hires' mouths. It is a very unique type of worker who thrives in unstructured work environments, and the data is clear: the majority of restorers are not that type of worker, especially during their first few weeks on the job.

Many respondents also felt ill-equipped to fulfill their job requirements, and wished their onboarding experience included more in-depth skills training, or opportunities to job shadow other team members. In particular, many workers complained about all the job software they were required to learn in order to do their job properly, and felt overwhelmed long after their training period had ended.

Unplanned, unstructured employee on-boarding has all the retention of a leaky bucket. Whatever you pour in will leak right out.

Scan to tweet!

> **It was great getting to know everyone and learning about the industry as I'd never worked in it before.**
>
> - Gen Z Office Administrator, Utah

It's important to note the workers who wished their onboarding experience had more job shadowing did not say "I wish I was thrown onto a job site and told I could ask the other technician there if I had any questions". This is insufficient, and does not equip the worker for long-term success. Instead, many respondents wished their "computer training" was combined with "real-world training", where they could first be taught information in a safe environment, and then see it put into practice out on the jobsite.

Workers do not want to work at a company where it feels like management and HR are "winging it", yet that is the first impression many workers are given during company onboarding.

Unplanned, unstructured training has the retention of a leaky bucket: whatever you pour in will leak right out. More important-ly, it leaves workers wondering, *"Is this the company's way of doing things, and if so, do I want to be here?"*

A Positive First Impression

Workers had a long list of improvements they'd like to see in their company's onboarding process, but there were also some no-table aspects of their first few weeks on the job that they didn't want to see changed. Given the importance of creating a strong first impression, it's worth doing a deep dive into what left new hires excited about their work environment, and optimistic about their future with their new employer.

According to the Restoration Workforce Survey, nothing cre-ated a stronger impression during the first few weeks on the job than positive interactions with other team members.

Considering how critical a positive team culture is to young work-ers, it's hardly surprising that being greeted by friendly faces and being given the opportunity to get to know new co-workers was what many new hires found most enjoyable. Likewise, if workers had negative interactions with colleagues during the first week, that also left a lasting impression on them.

Next, almost a quarter of restorers surveyed found the most ex-citing part about their first few weeks on the job to be the new

> 66
>
> **I loved the variety during my first few weeks, and be-ing able to get involved in things right from the get-go. I didn't feel like a number to my company.**
>
> - Millennial Technician, Florida
>
> 99

What Did You Enjoy About Your First Two Weeks?

Responses from the 2022 Restoration Workforce Survey

Learning New Skills

Team Member Interactions

Independence/Autonomy

Variety of Work

Structure

Office Staff
- 24%
- 5%
- 5%
- 3%
- 63%

Field Workers
- 28%
- 7%
- 17%
- 7%
- 41%

Managers
- 30%
- 6%
- 7%
- 9%
- 48%

skills they picked up and the rapid (not overwhelming) pace of learning. For those new to the industry, companies with structured, intentional training roadmaps left them feeling empowered and excited to bring what they were learning into the real world. One employee described their onboarding by saying "I loved learning everything that goes into restoration and how my role fit into that. I also had personal training from my manager every day, which went a long way."

There is a clear, natural throughline between the reason a worker decides to work for your company, and what fills them with the most enthusiasm and excitement during their first few weeks on the job. Is it a coincidence that the two most important factors to young people when selecting a workplace are team culture and growth opportunities, and the two things they enjoy most about their onboarding experience is team interactions and new skill development? Of course not. These workers came to your company looking for something very specific, and your training program gives them a clue as to whether they made the right choice or not.

Managers and leaders reading this, be aware of your own bias.

Many restorers grew up in an era that told them "the restoration industry is tough and unforgiving, and Day 1 on the job is your first taste of what's to come". These leaders might believe the only way to baptize a new employee is by fire, because after all "this is all I knew, and I turned out fine".

The data reveals that young workers have no patience for this approach. They want to know they're making the most of their time, and companies that cannot show they're providing what the worker is looking for will find themselves with a perpetual "Now Hiring" sign outside their front door.

Creating a Good Onboarding Experience

It's a candidate's market right now, and your candidates know it. If their onboarding experience does not show glimpses of what was promised during the interview stage, they will assume that the job will also not meet their expectations, and their time at your company will crash before it ever gets off the ground.

Employers that want to win with today's workforce need to radically alter their approach for this new generation of workers. Saying "it worked for me, so it will work for you" simply won't cut it anymore, and the leaders that ignore the facts and stick to old methods are doing so at the expense of their own success.

According to the data, here are some of the changes you need to incorporate into your onboarding process to properly train new hires, and show them you're serious about equipping them to succeed.

Give Your Workers Structure

New hires need to be provided with structure within the *first hour* on the job. This is your chance to infuse the worker with the assurance that their needs will be met. Then, and only then, can you begin to create a sense of enthusiasm for the job. New hires must know their company isn't just "winging it"; there's a plan in place to ensure they have the skills and information to succeed in their role. A few small changes can set a company up for success.

First, you need to communicate your company values. From the onset, your new hire should be given a sense of what is most

> 66
>
> **I wish I'd been trained in all the mitigation forms I'd have to deal with, and what the process was for emergency calls.**
>
> - Gen X Technician, Washington   99

important to your company: what behaviors you value, and why you all collectively wake up in the morning. As Chuck Violand, Principal at Violand Management told us, ideally this should be communicated from the owner of the company. "On the first day

Your values are guideposts for every piece of feedback you give your employees. Make sure they're well-understood.

Scan to tweet!

of employment, every effort should be made to have the owner of the company spend time with the new hire," Chuck says. "In very small companies, this might be the entire day. In larger companies, it should be at least the time required to cover the company's vision, mission, and core values." Your values are the foundation your company is built on, and this information will serve the employee in every aspect of their job. When they are unsure about how to proceed, they'll refer back to the company values, so these should be accessible and at the forefront of a new hire's mind. Organizations that truly model their values communicate them clearly, and call them out when they see them in action.

Likewise, these values are the guideposts for every corrective conversation you'll have with your staff, so new hires need to clearly understand what your company values, and what it doesn't.

Next, you need to build a culture of morning meetings. At this point, morning production meetings should be broadly adopted

> 66
>
> **Onboarding would have been more helpful if I was given specific processes for specific tasks I might encounter.**
>
> - Millennial Estimator, 99
>   California

across the industry, as this is an effective way to get everyone on the same page daily. This also provides structure and routine to your new hires from Day 1. The potential problem here lies with veteran workers who have no interest in changing their habits. Many of them might

Your company values are the compass that tell new hires what direction you're going in, and when they're going off-course.

simply say, "Yeah, I'm not coming to that." It will be tempting to let them off the hook, excusing their behavior as the way of the old guard. By doing so, you've not only made your operations worse in the short run, you've created a two-tier system where some staff follow the rules, and some don't. It doesn't take long before new hires begin to include themselves in that category, and you've once again allowed an unstructured work environment to flourish that repels young employees and creates consistent headaches for your management team. Nip this problem in the bud once and for all, and make morning meetings mandatory for all staff. Even if the meetings are shift-oriented and only take ten minutes, they will make a big difference in the productivity of your staff and will send the message to your new hires that you take proactive steps to eliminate chaos and bring them the structure they're looking for. If you're looking for tips on how to improve your morning meetings, check out the Morning Tech Meeting podcast from Blue Collar Nation.

Third, establish a routine of larger, company-wide gatherings.
Beyond the short morning meetings, it's critical you are checking in on employees, listening to their questions and resolving

> **❝**
> **I had no idea what was expected of me. I did not have a job title or description so I was not confident to approach tasks I didn't think were mine.**
>
> - Millennial Manager, Washington
> **❞**

pending issues at least monthly. New hires told us that few things leave a stronger positive impression than great interactions among team members during the first few weeks, so take advantage of this by creating structured monthly gatherings for the whole company. Use this opportunity to highlight the previous month's wins, recognize employees who went above and beyond, and remind staff of your company values. These 30 minutes can make a significant difference in a new hire's perception of the workplace, and determine whether or not they stick around for the long-haul.

Finally, you need to prioritize becoming a process-driven company. Employees want to be given the keys to succeed, and the number one request new hires had was more structure in their workplace. Companies that are serious about equipping and empowering workers have clearly documented the "way we do things here" for every role. Software tools like KnowHow, a hub for all of a company's processes, take this information and put it in the pocket or laptop of every employee, whether they're out on the jobsite or in the office. This does wonders for new hires, giving them a clear roadmap for being successfully onboarded and gaining the skills they need to do their job effectively. It also gives workers in the field confidence knowing that, even if they've never encountered a certain problem before, they have all the answers on their phone in a moment's notice. With an operating system like KnowHow, workers in any language can access your standard operating procedures, taking away variability and inconsistency from new hires and seasoned veterans.

Give Your Workers Sufficient Training

In the restoration industry, training is situationally driven and skills can't be taught all in one day. People learn by doing, and with such a wide variety of necessary skills it takes time for a new hire to feel sufficiently versed in every aspect of the job. However, that is no excuse for insufficient training. If management is too overwhelmed by the amount of training necessary, then you can bet new hires are equally overwhelmed. What new employees need in their earliest days with your company is guidance and reassurance that they will gain the competency required to succeed in their role. Here are some of the changes you need to make to ensure new hires consistently are equipped with the skills necessary to bring the most value to your company.

Especially for employees new to the restoration industry, your company onboarding should convince them they'll gain the compentency required to succeed in their role.

Scan to tweet!

First, document the competencies required for each role. Before any hire is made, you should know what skills you're looking for. Once that hire is brought onto the team, the critical job of ensuring they're competent in the areas you've designated begins. If you don't know what success looks like, you'll have a hard time equipping your employees to be successful. Before a worker completes their onboarding, their manager should

> 66
>
> **I wish I was given some sort of manual that would guide new hires on what to do. Instead I was handed a ton of jobs very quickly before I felt fully trained. Learning on the job was incredibly stressful.**
>
> - Gen X Project Manager, Florida 99

have an accurate understanding of what their strengths are, and where they still need development to meet the needs of the role they're in.

Second, define the roadmap for each role. If you know the skills each role needs, the next step is to create a clearly defined roadmap for how a new hire is going to gain those skills. Don't assume an employee is going to start Day 1 with a full toolbelt. Instead, define their development roadmap, from the "you're hired" handshake to their six-month review. Their first day on the job, put this roadmap in front of them and show them how you'll be equipping them with what they need to thrive in their role.

Third, take the time for your new hire to develop positive relationships. Positive interactions with other staff members go a long way in getting a new hire more comfortable in their environment. According to Chuck Violand, "because an employee's longevity with a company is closely tied to the relationships they establish within the first two weeks of employment, new hires should spend casual time with every member of their immediate team or department." Strike

Managers that pride themselves in how quickly they pick up the phone might be doing more harm than good.

while the iron is hot and remind new employees, especially young ones, that if they care about a strong team culture, they made the right decision in choosing to work for your company.

Finally, beware creating a culture of dependency. Too many workplaces send their new workers off to a jobsite and tell them just to call their supervisor if they've got any questions. This gives your new hire license to not seek out answers on their own, but instead rely on more experienced members of their team to fill any gaps they have. These interruptions exponentially increase as you bring on new team members, until you have a few critical "linchpins" your entire company is reliant on in order to complete a job successfully.

You need to equip every member of your team with the tools to solve problems as they come up.

> 66
> **I enjoyed learning all my company's processes during the first few weeks. I felt like I was building a good foundation for success.**
>
> - Baby Boomer Office 99
>   Administrator, Washington

This means ensuring they've got access to your company process library, and know how to use it when they encounter situations they haven't been in before.

Give Your Workers Autonomy

The Restoration Workforce Survey asked workers where they go to when they need answers, and almost half of them told us they call up their managers. Most companies are proud of this stat, but the truth is that it's a huge productivity loss. The mental habit being formed among workers is that if you don't know something, call your boss, interrupt their day, ask them to re-explain something, wait for a response, and *then* finish the job. This equates to hours of productivity lost each week.

51% of workers polled said that their managers get back to them within fifteen minutes.

If you think that's something worth bragging about, think about the awful implications of this. *"As a manager, I always pick up,"* you may say. This essentially turns the manager into a call center, instead of a valuable member of your team that has their own skills to bring to the company.

How many restoration owners and leaders hired managers so they could just answer worker questions all day? None.

Yet too many managers have sunk into this role, never giving any tasks of their own 100% focus because they're constantly getting interrupted by employees ill-equipped to solve problems themselves. How can your company expand if your managers are always running around doing the work you hired field technicians to do? The restoration industry has created umbilical cord relationships between workers and managers, and every time you hire a new worker, you are only draining your management resources.

Don't confuse what works in customer service with what works in worker-manager relationships. In the restoration industry, we have this mentality of "we always pick up our phones" because, when it comes to customers, we absolutely must. We are dealing with natural disasters that require instant attention, and cus-

---

66

I wish our owner wasn't such a micromanager. He is not open to new ways to complete documentation and create project transparency.

- Gen X Manager, Washington

99

tomers simply will not stand for a slow response time. But you shouldn't apply that mentality to your staff.

Even the military has evolved in this regard. There was a time when, in the midst of battle, if the enemy took down the general, the troops would scatter. But now, soldiers are trained in principles and tactics, and they know how to function as segments, independently solving problems as they arise.

> 66
> **The biggest thing I needed during my first two weeks were a clear path and direction on what I should be doing.**
>
> - Millennial Estimator, Utah 99

Many companies in the restoration industry misunderstand the key functions of management. Rather than being a 'walking Frequently-Asked-Questions machine', companies must standardize their 'way' doing things, freeing up managers for the work of management. As management guru Peter Drucker explained, managers' role is to define, optimize and manage *processes* and pursue growth initiatives for the company. Sadly, many managers find themselves as very well-paid adult babysitters.

Your job is not to be a surrogate parent to your employees. In doing so, you're devouring manager capacity and setting your employees up for disappointment. They become accustomed to instant answers, never learning to think for themselves. When the day comes that a manager isn't able to come through for them, the whole system breaks down. The employee feels abandoned, your manager feels like a failure, and the job doesn't get done.

Instead, equip employees with the ability to solve problems themselves, knowing their managers are there to support them, not do their work for them. Combining clearly defined process libraries with structured check-ins is the right balance of autonomy and syncing up. Employees know they are not left on their own if they get stuck, but are given freedom to figure things out on their own by consulting the company's SOP hub before bringing in other colleagues or managers. You as a manager are still touching base with them daily, and have a clear line of sight on if they're thriving, or if they're struggling in their early days and need more support.

The goal of onboarding is about setting your new hires up for success.

Workers want to know they made the right decision in choosing to join your company, and you've got an opportunity to get your relationship off on the right foot with an intentional onboarding process.

The restoration industry is an industry built on chaos, but today's workers have no tolerance for unstructured, chaotic environments. Companies that succeed in providing clear roadmaps to equip new team members will find themselves retaining the high-quality candidates they attracted during the hiring process, and turning B-players into A-players with development programs that give workers the skills they need, regardless of their starting point. Combine this with process libraries in every worker's pocket and structured meetings, and you've got a training program that not only finds diamonds in the rough, but makes diamonds out of the rough too.

⩊≡ Key Takeaways: Chapter 3

- ⊘ 75% of new hires say they see room for improvement with their company's onboarding processes, with 22% specifically asking for more structure
- ⊘ Workers in every role most enjoy getting to meet new team members during their onboarding. 25% of employees said the most fulfilling part was learning the new skills they'd need to do their jobs
- ⊘ To create an effective onboarding program, leaders need to provide structure, sufficient training, and a sense of autonomy
- ⊘ An overdependence on managers to solve problems is limiting worker capacity and preventing companies from growing efficiently
- ⊘ If new hires do not get what they need during their first two weeks on the job, they are far less likely to stick around to see if things will improve

4

The Best Parts About Working in Restoration

CHAPTER 4

What's To Love?

The Best Parts About Working in Restoration

The Great Resignation has proven that today's worker believes they hold the cards for the type of work they do, and what type of work is, frankly, beneath them.

If that's the case, many restoration owners may look down at the Category 3 water loss surrounding their work boots and say "Well then, who on earth would want to do this for a living?"

Is the restoration industry doomed by a generation afraid to get its hands dirty? Are there any redeemable qualities to an industry built on cleaning up other people's messes?

The implications of these questions go far beyond selling the restoration industry to young workers. Leaders and owners that fundamentally don't understand why their workers have chosen to work in restoration, what they truly enjoy about their day-to-day jobs, and why they wake up in the morning have no chance at creating a work environment that gives these employees the fulfillment they're looking for. To retain talented staff over the long haul, you must understand what are the characteristics of the job that matters most to them, that contributes to them loving what they do.

> **66**
> **I love working with new clients and getting positive feedback from clients when we do great work.**
>
> - Gen X Manager, Washington
> **99**

In contrast to the fears of the restoration owner standing in six inches of dirty water, there are some unique aspects of the restoration industry that workers don't just enjoy, they love. Each role has specific elements they enjoy more than others, and managers that win with today's workforce know what these are, and how to take advantage of them to create a positive work environment for each staff member.

If you're a restoration leader looking to keep your best workers excited and motivated to come to work every day, here's a guide-map to the best parts about working in the restoration industry, in their own words.

The Most Fulfilling Part of the Job

Employees across the board, in every role, said one single factor had greater influence over whether they found their job fulfilling than anything else: other people.

〽️ Facts at a Glance: Chapter 4

35%
of workers say the best part about the restoration industry is working with others

50%
How much more valuable team interactions are to Gen Z employees compared to Baby Boomers

19%
of field techs think the most rewarding part about being in restoration in helping others

---

What Are the Most Enjoyable Parts of Your Job?

Responses from the 2022 Restoration Workforce Survey

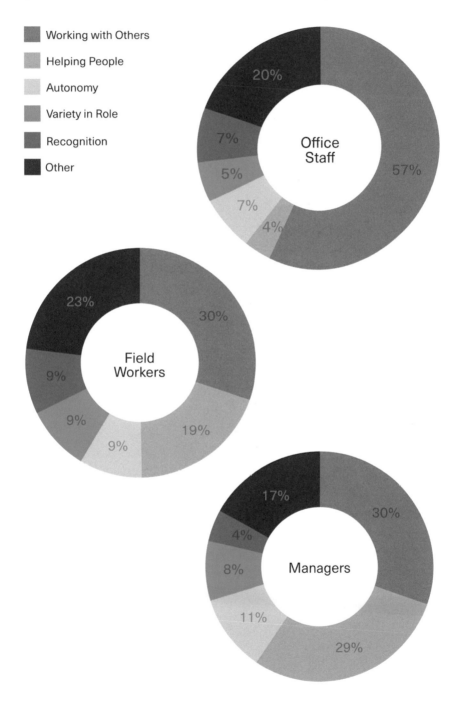

This was universal between office staff, field workers, and managers, yet it clearly had the biggest impact on those in the office. 57% of these employees said the most enjoyable part of their job on any given day is being shoulder-to-shoulder with their colleagues, tackling challenges together and enjoying the atmosphere along the way. Similarly, field workers loved getting to meet new people every day, and working alongside teammates to solve problems and make a difference. As one technician described, "I love working with other employees, creating very happy customers, and encountering new and interesting projects every day."

The Percentage of Employees Who Listed "Working with Others" at the Best Part About Restoration

Responses to the 2022 Restoration Workforce Survey

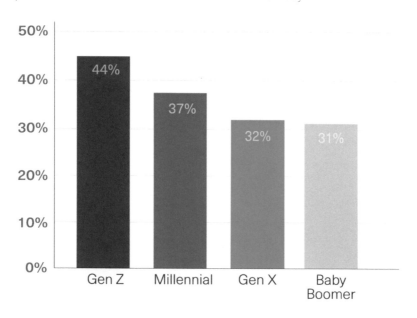

Importantly, this fulfillment from working with other people is only growing among younger generations. 30% of Baby Boomers stated that working with others was the most enjoyable part of their job, but this steadily increased among each age group until it reached 44% from Gen Z workers. Clearly, the desire for a positive team atmosphere and interactions with others isn't a trend that will phase out. The data tells us that it's here to stay, and industry leaders must cultivate more of it in order to retain young workers.

> 66
> **The best part is working with homeowners in their time of need and sending a great crew to do the job.**
>
> - Millennial Manager, Wisconsin
> 99

Among field workers and managers, another extremely fulfilling aspect of being in restoration is the ability to help others, often on the worst days of their lives. In fact, no word appeared more in the response to this question than the word "help". As this Project Manager put it, "the best part is working with homeowners in their time of need, and sending a great crew to do the job".

What's remarkable is when you combine this information with the reasons candidates accepted their current role, discussed in Chapter 2. Of the 48% joining the restoration industry for the first time, none mentioned they did so because they wanted to help others. Clearly, the impact a good restoration team can have

> 66
> **It's always rewarding to have a customer appreciate what I'm doing for them even when their situation is not the greatest.**
>
> - Millennial Technician, Washington
> 99

on a customer's life is an unknown quantity entering into the restoration industry, but it quickly makes itself apparent (especially to field workers and managers). This means that one of the most fulfilling aspects of working in the restoration industry catches many workers by surprise, and it isn't until they're on the ground that they can see the impact of their work, and how much of a difference it makes to customers.

Restoration managers and leaders should be salivating over found money here.

In an industry that looks unglamorous from an outside perspective, you've got 20% of your frontline field technicians saying they find tremendous fulfillment in the difference they can make in customers' lives, and feeling personally responsible for restoring somebody's home back to a great condition. With more workers today looking for meaning and purpose in their work, the restoration industry has the unique ability to provide a tangible "before & after" on the impact each worker can make. Talk about feeling like you can make a difference in the lives of others!

Good Days vs Bad Days

Similarly, it's important to know what causes an employee to clock out of work with a smile on their face, regardless of the role they're in. If each worker is looking in different directions to

> 66
>
> **I love our current team. We make the most out of every job, stressful or not.**
>
> - Millennial Technician, Washington   99

Restorers often see people on their worst days, and help them rebuild their lives.

receive fulfillment from their job, the question must be asked: did they succeed?

Do they go home feeling accomplished, excited for another day? Or do they leave work battered and bruised, unsure of how long they can postpone their inevitable last day. The answers provide an important glimpse into what workers feel is most valuable, and where they get their sense of accomplishment (or lack thereof) from.

We asked the restoration workforce what causes them to have a great day, and more than any other response, workers told us their happiness was directly tied to how productive they felt on any given day. This was especially true among office staff, who love connecting with their colleagues, but not at the expense of a hard day's work.

For field workers, the desire for productivity was just as strong, but their success metric for a good day vs a bad one came down to how many surprises popped up throughout the day as a result of poor planning. Clearly, these workers have been burned so many times by materials not being delivered, scope creep,

> **66**
>
> **My favorite part of the day is our lunch break. The boss always provides a healthy lunch for us from Subway.**
>
> - Millennial Estimator, California **99**

co-worker no-shows and more, that just getting through a day without a bunch of new fires emerging is itself a good day. As one worker put it, "The best days are when I'm given a good scope and the tools to be able to complete the job properly". Something that seems so simple in theory tends to be remarkably difficult in practice, but these warning signs should not be ignored by managers: workers want to do their jobs well, and until managers can do *their* jobs well, their workers are going to go home frustrated and angry, instead of fulfilled.

Creating the Best Place to Work

In a leaky-bucket industry with high turnover, how can industry leaders use this data to their advantage? We've learned that if the younger generations aren't enjoying the job, they tend to leave. So, the goal is to create an environment that maximizes employee enjoyment. The good news is that almost every one of the factors mentioned by workers in the Restoration Workforce Survey is well within company control, so proactive managers have

> **66**
>
> **The best days are the ones where I'm productive and mark lots of tasks off my to-do list, especially when it keeps everyone else updated and happy. If my co-workers are productive as well, that's a bonus.**
>
> - Gen Z Office Administrator, **99**
>   Utah

lots of tools in their toolbelt.

What Are the Main Causes of Good Days?

Responses from the 2022 Restoration Workforce Survey

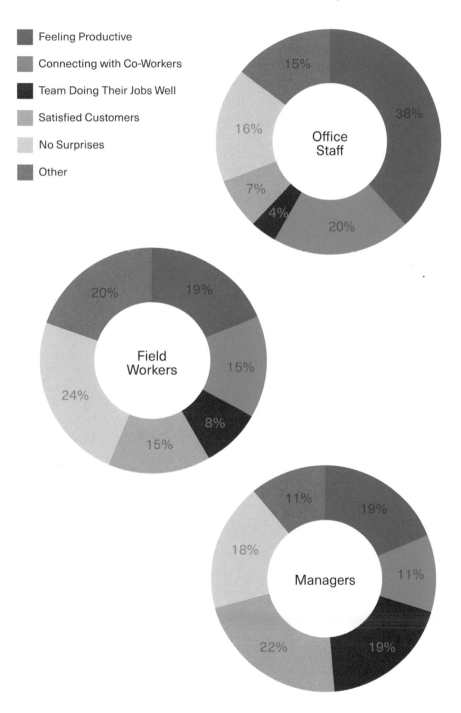

Legend:
- Feeling Productive
- Connecting with Co-Workers
- Team Doing Their Jobs Well
- Satisfied Customers
- No Surprises
- Other

Office Staff
- 38%
- 20%
- 4%
- 7%
- 16%
- 15%

Field Workers
- 19%
- 15%
- 8%
- 15%
- 24%
- 20%

Managers
- 19%
- 11%
- 19%
- 22%
- 18%
- 11%

Eliminate Process Breakdowns that Kill Productivity

Let's start with the most obvious problem first: workers are happiest when they feel productive, yet many of them run into routine barriers to that productivity. For field workers, that's showing up to a jobsite without the necessary materials, or being surrounded by poorly trained colleagues who don't know what they're supposed to be doing (more on this in the next chapter). For office workers, this is an unclear picture on what they're supposed to be doing on any given day, or numerous interruptions that keep them from doing the work they need to get done. As one office worker told us, "A good day is a day with no phone calls, no issues on jobs, and no distractions from me completing my to-dos".

Management needs to surround workers with the structure and communication necessary to get these workers to their desired productivity state. When workers arrive on-site and the scope of work has not been clearly defined, that is a process breakdown. When an office administrator can't complete her to-dos because she keeps getting phone calls from confused techs in the field, that is a process breakdown. The onus is on management to do the hard work of defining company processes and keeping them at the forefront of employees minds so they are not being killed by a thousand papercuts throughout the day and going home frustrated because they couldn't complete the simple task they were hired to do.

Encourage Team Culture

There are countless ways you can strengthen the connection co-workers feel with each other, and most of them simply re-

> 66
>
> **The best days at work are the days when everything goes exactly according to plan.**
>
> - Millennial Project Manager, Nebraska
>
> 99

What Do You Currently Enjoy That You Don't Want to See Changed?

Responses from the 2022 Restoration Workforce Survey

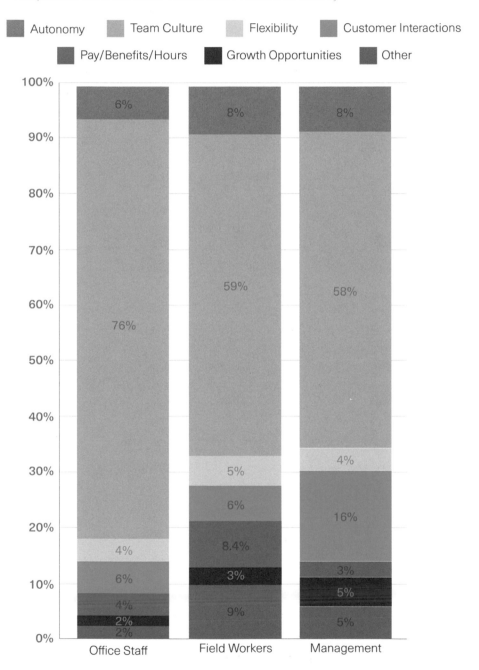

quire intentionality. Learning about your staff, initiating weekly check-ins, and acknowledging traits and personalities go a long way and cost the company nothing. So, you must create opportunities for these interactions, and you'll want the interactions to feel organic.

In order to build positive relationships among your staff, give them opportunities to get to know one another.

Stop and consider the members of your current team. What rituals could you instill that would bring them together? Maybe a monthly flag football game, or a street hockey tournament. Order pizzas on Fridays, and bring in donuts on Mondays - find little opportunities for colleagues to connect over lunch. Remember and acknowledge birthdays, recognize excellent work, and show concern—not just anger—when someone slips up.

> 66
>
> **I love my co-workers, flexibility when I need time off, and company parties.**
>
> - Millennial Office Administrator, Pennsylvania 99

In short, pay attention to your staff and provide small additions that make work a more pleasant experience. It's easy to pretend that these environments don't matter, but when you are drowning in employee turnover, there's no ignoring the wants and needs of your workforce. According to the data, today's workers continually choose careers that value human connection; it's up to you to decide if your workplace is one of them.

Invest In Your Staff's Soft Skills

It's tempting to believe that, as a company owner, you have little to no control over your field techs' customer interactions, but that's narrow-minded thinking. Just as you train your employees in necessary job skills, you can train them in customer service. Many blue-collar workers aren't particularly comfortable inter-

Connecting over sports and food provides a great opportunity for co-workers to strengthen their bonds with each other in a more relaxed environment.

acting with customers, and therefore they need to see strong leaders model this behavior for them.

Previously, KnowHow analyzed over 1,000 one-star customer reviews in the restoration industry. 11% of those reviews cited bad customer service, and another 7.6% pointed to wild, unethical contractor behavior. The underlying issue is that many company leaders don't realize the importance of soft skills training when it comes to their frontline workers. Dan Cassara, Chief Executive Officer of CORE Group told us, "I cannot stress enough that you've got to invest in your frontline staff. They're the front door to your business." Your workers will likely be the only reflection of the company your customers will see, so it's critical they know how to make customers feel comfortable and calm.

> 66
> **The people I work with are awesome, and I get to speak with new people every day out in the field.**
>
> - Gen Z Project Manager, Maryland 99

This is doubly true because workers have told us there are few things that feel more fulfilling than seeing a customer with a smile on their face at the end of a job. By investing in your workers' ability to assuage the concerns of a new customer and guide them through the process from chaos back to order, you not only strengthen your company's perception among clients, you strengthen your worker's loyalty to your business. Every call you receive is an opportunity to create an amazing, fulfilling experience for workers and customers alike. Alternatively, poor customer service can pour gasoline on an already blazing fire. Set standards for how your employees should carry themselves when wearing your company brand, demonstrate how to meet those standards, and hold them to it. Your customers, and employees, will thank you for it.

Your frontline staff are the front door to your business, and the face of your company to your customer.

Scan to tweet!

Encourage Responsible Autonomy

One last thing workers consistently valued was the sense of autonomy they felt when out on a jobsite, or managing their own task list. This means that company leaders must be intentional about putting the right infrastructure in place that creates autonomy, yet maintains accountability. The last thing a worker wants is to be standing in a customer's house, knee-deep in a pool of water, and not know what to do because their manager told

> 66
> **I enjoy the positive environment and how my team trusts me to do my thing and bring them clients and losses.**
>
> - Gen X Salesperson, Oklahoma
> 99

them they'd get to water damage training later. At the same time, as we discussed in Chapter 3, workers just being told to hop on the phone if they ever have any questions is just as damaging for the health of your business, and happiness of your worker.

What's the right balance? It all comes back to sufficient, structured training.

The first and most impactful way to train your employees is to arm them with instantaneous access to the company's processes, workflows, and procedures through a software tool like Know-How. With all the information in one place, there is no reason a skilled worker can't handle any situation within the company's purview.

> 66
> **I have a lot of freedom and flexibility. I can make mistakes as long as we learn from them.**
>
> - Millennial Manager, Lousiana 99

Secondly, company leaders must continually push company values. Any worker discipline or positive feedback should all be rooted in your company values. Hammer these ideas home, so that your employees can refer back to them when they need clarity. This is how you ensure your staff knows what is expected of them.

Additionally, invest in teaching problem-solving skills, so that when an employee has an issue, they have the resources to figure it out on their own. You don't want all your workers regularly calling their managers, or worse—*waiting* until they hear back from their manager.

And finally, instill a sense of ownership-thinking. Leaders should model this behavior by doing—cleaning up at the end of the day, taking care of the equipment, and being mindful of their appearance. Acknowledge workers when they demonstrate ownership,

> **In our company, employees are empowered at each level to solve whatever problems come up.**
>
> - Millennial Estimator, Oklahoma

making it clear your company values employees who wear the success of their company as if it's their own. You might consider investing in quality, attractive company apparel that your staff would take pride in wearing. When your employees are proud of their company, they are more likely to represent it well.

With these pieces in place, you can foster a strong sense of autonomy among your staff without just letting employees go rogue and solve problems however they'd like. Too many employers make the mistake of loosening the reins before they've set up the necessary structure to encourage both autonomy and accountability.

Restoration companies that get this balance right will find themselves attracting workers who take ownership in the work they do, and feeling empowered as they get there.

When restoration owners read the headlines about workers walking out of jobs they don't find fulfilling, they may feel like the deck is stacked against them. The Restoration Workforce Survey proves them dead wrong. There are certainly challenges as we'll get to next, but leaders are fooling themselves if they don't think there are inherently rewarding aspects of the restoration industry that they can take advantage of to increase employee satisfaction and attract new workers to the restoration industry. From the feeling of tackling challenges with teammates to helping people on their worst days, there is a gold mine of opportunity to make every staff member's job experience more richly rewarding for managers willing to take advantage of the trends, motivations, and values of the next generation of workers.

☷ Key Takeaways: Chapter 4

- ⊘ 57% of office staff say the best part about their jobs is being able to work with others every day. 30% of field workers and managers agreed

- ⊘ Likewise, 59% of all workers say they enjoy their relationship with their co-workers and would not want it to change

- ⊘ More than office staff, field workers and managers feel great fulfillment in the way their work helps others

- ⊘ More than anything, workers in the field say a good day comes down to a day without any surprises

- ⊘ To create an enjoyable work environment, leaders must eliminate process breakdowns, encourage team culture, invest in your staff's soft skills and encourage responsible autonomy

5

The Worst Parts About
Working in Restoration

CHAPTER 5

What's To Hate?

The Worst Parts About Working in
Restoration

If the restoration industry has some very unique positive elements to it, it's safe to assume there are also particular elements of the job that wear on workers, testing their patience
and their commitment to the industry.

Considering the frequency at which today's modern worker is
taking a step back to reconsider his or her career choices, it's imperative that managers are well aware of the worst parts about
the restoration industry, from the perspective of the worker, so
they can attempt to mitigate problems.

And what you'll find in this chapter is particularly surprising: very,
very few of the complaints you're about to read mention anything
inherent to the restoration industry. In fact, out of our hundreds
of survey responses, the word 'poop' only came up once!

Instead, you'll find a long list of grievances that managers have
lots of control over. This is good news, because employees can
always tell the difference between "this is just a hard part about
the job" and "this could be better if the people around me were
more competent/intentional".

66

The workload is a lot for what you get paid. It can be very unmotivating if you are on call and work 50 hours a week to take home less than $1k after taxes.

- Gen Z Project Manager, Maryland

99

Today's worker does not demand an easy job, but The Great Resignation has proven that they will not sit by indefinitely while the worst parts of their experience go unaddressed.

Managers that want to attract and retain this new generation of workers need to work actively to identify the most frustrating aspects of a job and take clear, intentional steps to remove barriers and impediments where they can. Not dealing with obvious problems is a surefire way to bleed quality workers left and right.

The path to a better workplace for you and your workers is not by avoiding pain, it's by dealing with it head on. Here are the worst parts of the restoration industry, from the perspective of its workforce:

The Least Fulfilling Part of the Job

Out of all the different aspects of the restoration industry, what are the most soul-crushing? Which tasks leave workers going home feeling frustrated and defeated, unsure if they're cut out for this industry or not?

📈 Facts at a Glance: Chapter 5

84%	16%	24%
of workers say the worst part of their job was not a task inherent to the industry	of restorers say the worst part of their job is tedious, mindless tasks that seem disconnected from the big picture	of field techs said team members dropping the ball was their biggest source of frustration

About 16% of workers surveyed mentioned a specific job function of theirs that exhausted them. For example, many managers said anything related to collecting payment for services rendered was particularly painful for them, which is unsurprising. No one signs up for the restoration industry because they like hounding insurance companies to pay up. Many other managers cited the constant hiring process as a tiring, defeating element of working in the restoration industry.

There's a clear disconnect in the restoration industry between the work that's being done, and the greater good it's accomplishing.

Scan to tweet!

But the vast, vast majority of workers in the restoration industry (84% by comparison) cited aspects of the job that were not simply a task, like collections or hiring, as the least fulfilling. Almost all of these issues are completely addressable, if managers are willing to do something about it.

16% of workers pointed to the tedious amount of paperwork they're required to do on any given day, with office workers saying this was by far the worst element of their job. As one employee put it "I often feel like I'm doing things that don't move the needle in any way". Others often used the terms "busywork", "bureaucratic" and "redundant" in describing the work they had to do.

> 66
> **The repetitiveness of this job can be very disheartening.**
> 99
> - Millennial Estimator, New Jersey

It's clear there's a disconnect here between the work that's being input, and its relationship to the vision and mission of the company. If workers don't understand how their tasks are contributing to the overall goals of the company, they're either doing the wrong tasks, or management has done a poor job communicating why the work they do is important. Additionally, if your company is using outdated methods of data entry and project management, you could be inflicting unnecessary pain on your workers.

For field workers specifically, the high workload and being on-call was particularly draining. Missing birthday parties, date nights with the spouse, or the big game because of the industry they've chosen is particularly defeating, and few people are enthusiastic to give away control of their schedule for years or decades of their lives. Given the restoration industry's high turnover rate, it may feel unavoidable that field workers will always have to bear the brunt of this, but if you've read this book this far, you should believe otherwise.

You've got specific, tangible actions you can take to increase your company's ability to attract and retain top workers, and by not doing so you are testing your current staff's ability to feel

What is the Least Fulfilling Aspect of Your Role?

Responses from the 2022 Restoration Workforce Survey

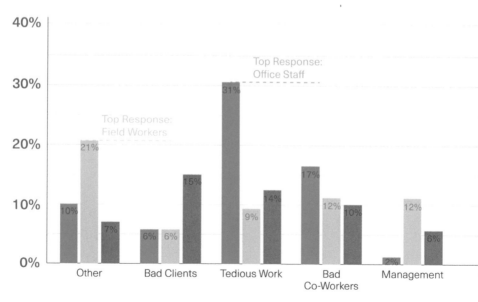

overworked for months or years on end. What if the 17% of your staff that feel exhausted because of their insane schedule finally handed in their two weeks notice and walked away? You'd best believe it might push the other 83% of your staff over the edge too.

The onus is on you to identify the ways you can relieve this pressure before it's too late.

It's also important to recognize in this data the influence that a bad work environment has on employee happiness. The flip side of the coin we discussed in the previous chapter, the same co-workers that can cause an employee to leave the jobsite excited about their workplace can leave them frustrated and angry if the environment is negative.

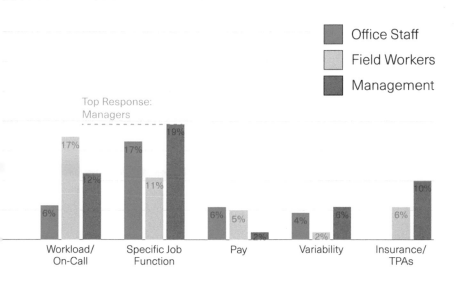

Considering the immense pressures on field techs, from angry clients to insurance (both of whom also made the list of Least Fulfilling Aspects of the restoration industry), companies should take a proactive role in developing a strong sense of camaraderie in the field.

Restoration is a tense, stressful job—not unlike that of first-responders. Field techs are called into chaotic situations and expected to remedy them quickly. Consider the potential repercussions if two field techs—addressing circuitry problems in a home severely damaged by a hurricane—don't trust each other. No matter how skilled they are, if they cannot communicate well, the stakes are life and death.

> 66
>
> **I feel like the only female in a male-dominated industry. I can get walked on sometimes.**
>
> - Gen Z Office Administrator, 99
>   Wisconsin

Firefighters are renowned for respecting their fellow workers. Each station is a family. Field techs may not need to be a "band of brothers," but management should place heavy emphasis in training workers and finding opportunities for their field staff to build bonds with each other.

The work these frontline techs do is too important to leave their interactions with co-workers to chance.

The Main Causes of Frustration

We now know the primary factors that leave workers unfulfilled, but of equal importance is understanding the main things that drive an employee crazy. If unfulfillment is a slow burn, frustration is 'in your face', a problem that needs to be addressed in the short term. If ignored, these lead to bad attitudes, passive aggression, outright aggression, and a host of other issues that will degrade morale and cause employees to eventually decide your work culture is not for them.

On a homeowner's worst day, they need a unified, aligned team coming together to help them rebuild their lives.

Chief among the things that grate on workers in every role was team members letting them down. From a poorly defined scope of work to other staff members being bottlenecks, the responses to this question were colorful, to say the least. As one worker put it, "when someone else doesn't do their job correctly, it directly affects my ability to do my job well".

It's obvious that part of the frustration here is that most workers know it doesn't *have* to be this way. "If management did a better job training new hires, or vetting candidates," they might say to themselves, "then I'd be able to finish this project on time."

> 66
>
> **It's very frustrating when people don't complete the work that needs to be completed and my next steps depend on them. Lack of preparedness and communication are a huge problem here.**
>
> - Gen X Manager, Washington
>
> 99

One of the primary roles of management is to remove barriers in front of their reports so they can get as much horsepower out of their staff as possible. When management fails to do this task, the result is workers turning on each other - pointing the finger when they can't get the job done properly. As we read in the last chapter, many workers just want to be able to put in a hard day's work and know they made an impact in the life of a customer. When team members cut corners or act selfishly, it not

What are the Main Causes of Frustration at Work?

Responses from the 2022 Restoration Workforce Survey

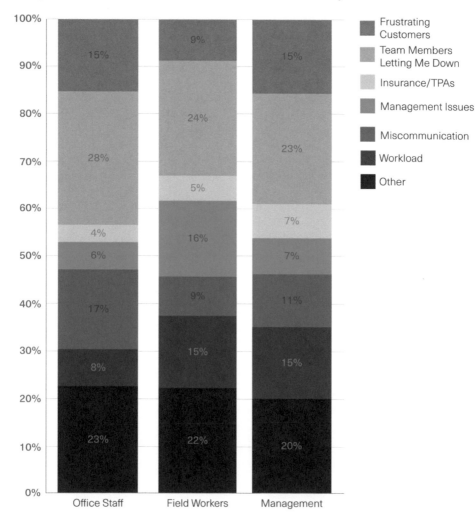

only slows down a job, it also obstructs their ability to feel deep meaning and fulfillment from the work they do. It's no wonder workers can only take so much of that feeling before they decide to move to a company with a better training program and higher standards for all its staff.

It's also important to identify one major difference between field workers and other roles in this category: how often they cited management issues as the biggest cause of frustration at work. According to the Restoration Workforce Survey, field workers are 167% more likely to complain about management than their co-workers in the office. Certainly, the same personality-type that values autonomy might chafe at their manager, but it's the responsibility of leadership to learn how to work well with all their staff members, and considering the importance of the field tech role, the consequences of getting this wrong can be severe.

When team members cut corners or act selfishly, it not only slows down the job, but also obstructs their ability to find fulfillment in work

Scan to tweet!

> 66
> **When other team members don't complete their tasks fully or are slow to bring something over the finish line, we all suffer.**
>
> - Millennial Office Administrator, Pennsylvania
> 99

Bridging the Gap

As we've discovered, if today's worker's frustration is mounting and they don't see signs of things turning around, they'll take their skills elsewhere. Just as employers must double-down on the most fulfilling aspects of working in restoration, they must also be ruthlessly targeted on eliminating or mitigating its most unfulfilling aspects. Some of the frustrations discussed are inherent to the job. For example, if the boss has issues with the pace of approvals in the insurance industry, they're going to have to go to the back of a very large line. But factors such as bad teammates, management conflicts, miscommunication and workload are all addressable, if managers are willing to do the hard work.

> 66
>
> **My work can feel very monotonous at times.**
>
> - Gen Z Technician,
>   Idaho
>
> 99

What was the root cause of most of the problems employees complained about? Poor communication.

While some workers clearly mentioned communication issues

Workers that don't know how their daily tasks contribute to the big picture are likely to feel their work is unimportant and mundane.

as their biggest grievance, many others pointed to their down-stream effects, such as conflicts with management, being let down by teammates, and more.

A lack of communication creates problems that manifest itself in every aspect of work, and dealing with only the symptoms, as opposed to the root cause, is like playing wack-a-mole: there's always another one that pops-up.

Instead, there are three specific areas you can target in your communication to eliminate the majority of the complaints voiced in this chapter.

First, you need to properly communication your vision and mission. As we discussed in the previous chapter, there's a significant number of restorers who find tremendous fulfillment in being able to help turn somebody's life around after a tragedy. Your management team should make it crystal clear to every worker how the work they're doing, whether that's cleaning up

Percent of Workers Who Would Be "Very Disappointed" if Their Company Closed Tomorrow

Responses from the 2022 Restoration Workforce Survey

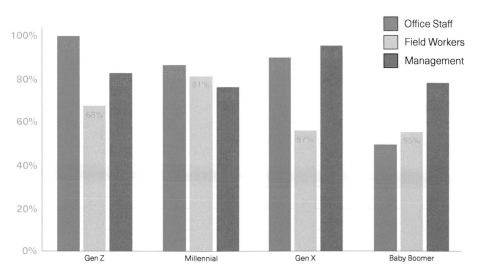

sewage or meeting insurance requirements in the office, fulfills your company mission and improves the life of a real person going through a really hard time.

In the 1960s, NASA was on a full-on sprint to put the first man on the moon. Every person there, in every role, understood how the work they did factored into the organization's overall mission.

At one point, in 1961, United States President John F. Kennedy was touring NASA's facilities when he ran into a janitor that was working well into the night. "Why are you working so late?" he asked the janitor. "Well, Mr. President," the janitor responded, "I'm helping put a man on the moon."

Every person in that organization knew they played a special and important role in achieving the organization's overall success. It's incumbent on you as a leader to communicate the grander vision behind the work your company does, and how it affects every role. With so many workers believing the tasks they're doing are just busywork, without a connection to the higher goals of the company, it's no wonder that teammates begin to let each other down as they start questioning "what's the point of doing all this anyway?"

Second, you need to clearly and consistently communicate the expectations you have for each employee. It should be obvious by now that when businesses neglect to properly communicate the company's values and priorities, everybody suffers. If bad apples on your team start spoiling the enthusiasm and passion of your best workers, you have a true nightmare scenario that needs to be addressed immediately.

> 66
>
> **Why can't people just do the job they were hired to do?**
>
> - Millennial Manager, Missouri 99

Behavior such as corner cut-

In the 1960s, everyone at NASA, from the astronauts to the janitors, knew the mission they were on and how the work they did contributed to accomplishing that mission.

ting or no shows, especially among full-time staff is unacceptable, and management needs to take a heavy hand to correct this. If this is the result of the worker not knowing what they're expected to do, take this as a lesson for both them and you. Your management team failed to clearly communicate what it is your company values, and the behaviors that you hold most supreme in your organization. Don't assume every new staff member has the same set of priorities that you do - the onus is on your team to create a plan to make it crystal clear to each team member what is expected of them, and what they'll be measured by. Identify where you saw evidence of behavior that was out of alignment

> 66
>
> **When people don't respect the processes that are put in place, it makes it that much harder for everyone else on the team.**
>
> - Millennial Office Administrator, Pennsylvania 99

with your values, and ensure they know that "going forward", this behavior won't be tolerated.

If the employee is well aware of what the expectations are, but is not interested in pulling their weight, you cannot let them drag the rest of your staff down with them. Though beginning the hiring process all over again is exhausting, you are gambling with your best talent if you believe not addressing employees with a bad attitude won't have downstream effects that will make life significantly harder for you and your team.

Finally, make a concerted effort to slow down and communicate intentionally. When one worker mentions how frustrating it is to show up on site without the correct materials or a scope of work provided, it's easy to see that as a mistake that could happen to any fast-paced organization. When dozens and dozens of workers are describing the exact same scenario, it's obvious there's a bigger communication problem in the restoration industry that needs to be addressed.

Restoration companies need a single source of truth that every worker can turn to if they have questions.

Scan to tweet!

As Phillip Rosebrook, Partner at Business Mentors told us, "Employees in the restoration industry are too often sent to jobs without proper expectations for the scope of work, or details other than a name, job number, and address. This is a function of incomplete or non-existent work orders with information on

66

I shouldn't be sent to a job with no scope of work and no idea regarding what I'm supposed to be doing.

- Gen Z Technician, Oklahoma

99

what has been done on the job to-date, and the condition of the jobsite."

The restoration industry is built upon the urgency and speediness of responses. The nature of this work can make thorough communication difficult - if not impossible. This is why value must be placed on clear, consistent communication at the outset.

Workers told us they get most of their information from managers on a need-to-know basis, either through fragmented text messages, e-mails, or second-hand from other restorers. This makes communication breakdowns inevitable.

Companies should have a single-source of truth that every worker knows to turn to if they've got questions. Not sure what we're supposed to be doing on the job today? Open up the work order. Forget how to properly Don & Doff PPE? Check our guide in our process manager.

> 66
> **It's frustrating dealing with poor leadership from upper management.**
> - Millennial Project Manager, 99
>   Lousiana

Combine this with consistent checkpoints throughout the week between management and staff as discussed in previous chapters, and your odds of a worker showing up unprepared without any of the right materials or prerequisites complete have gone down dramatically. If the goal is to eliminate the barriers that prevent staff from using their full skillset to move the needle for the company and accomplish your mission, you can easily make marked improvements in this area just by building established and consistent lines of communication into your company workflow.

No job is always glamorous, and this is doubly true of the industry that's been tasked with cleaning up after a disaster. But that doesn't mean bad attitudes and a poor employee retention rate are inevitable. The majority of the problems workers cited with the restoration industry are well within a manager's control to target and address. Yes, the industry is fast-paced, and leaders feel like they're always under water (literally, at times!) but that is no excuse for allowing the experience for workers to be worse than it needs to be.

The key to ensuring employees don't exit your organization prematurely is in the hands of one group: your management team.

Which brings us to our final, and most important chapter...

Want an exclusive presention of the most relevant insights from this book for your management team?

Limited spots are available for an exclusive training session featuring the most valuable insights from the Restoration Workforce Survey, and the impact it will have on your company's ability to attract and retain top talent.

Scan this QR Code for more info!

≣ Key Takeaways: Chapter 5

⊘ 84% of restorers said the least fulfilling aspects of their job were not tasks inherent to the restoration industry, but instead were internal dynamics that could be targeted and addressed

⊘ 16% of workers said the worst part of their job was doing meaningless, tedious work. Leaders need to reconnect the tasks of every team member to the broader mission of the company.

⊘ Overall, the biggest source of frustration among all employees was feeling like team members let them down

⊘ By focusing on communicating company values, communicating employee expectations, and communicating intentionally, management can set the bar for all staff and give them the tools to be able to work unobstructed

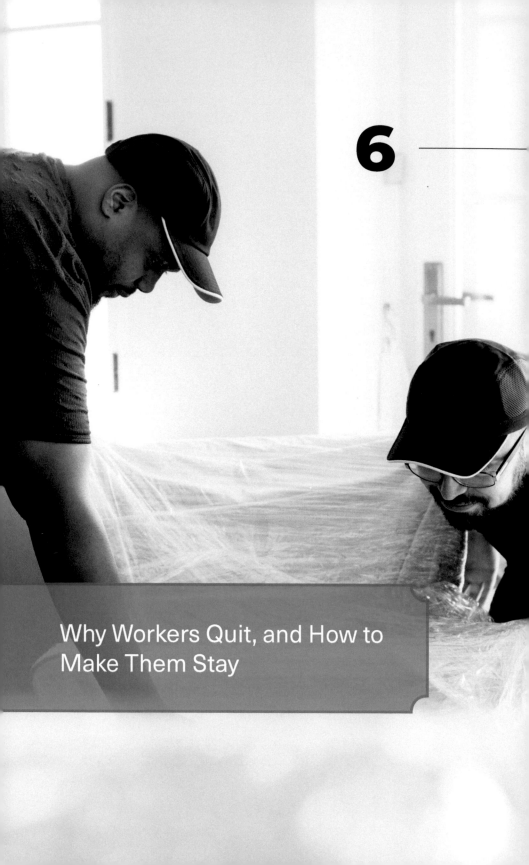

6

Why Workers Quit, and How to Make Them Stay

CHAPTER 6

That's It - I Quit!

Why Workers Quit and How to Make Them Stay

You're reading this because your workers quit more frequently than you think they should, or you're nervous resignations are coming and you don't know how to avoid them.

What the Restoration Workforce Survey has made abundantly clear is that the single biggest factor that contributes to workers quitting is your management team's management. Everything, from how you onboard employees, to how you communicate and enforce company values, either builds loyalty in your employees throughout the craziness of the industry, or edges them closer towards throwing their hands up and walking out the door

Why do restoration workers quit?

On behalf of the overwhelming majority of survey respondents, we can say with certainty that workers quit because of poor management.

A decision to quit is the sum total of hundreds of interactions a worker has with their individual manager on a weekly basis in which they experience behaviors, attitudes, habits and responses that are negative. The cumulative weight of these decisions on the part of management and leadership push people out the door.

Let us make one thing abundantly clear: based on the largest data set ever collected on the restoration workforce, the chasm between workers and managers is bigger than you think, and it's your job to fix it.

On a broader scale, the worker revolt we're seeing during this Great Resignation is a revolt against management, and the Restoration Workforce Survey has narrowed in on how this dynamic has manifested itself in the restoration industry. We've known this for a while, but only now are we experiencing the full watershed moment. In Gallup's comprehensive 2015 study, they found

📈 **Facts at a Glance: Chapter 6**

21%
of restorers say good people leave their company because of problems with management

70%
of workers listed tangible ways they'd like their manager to change his/her approach

59%
of field workers did not describe their relationship with their manager as great

a harsh truth: 75% of people quit their job to "get away from their manager". Meaning, the number one reason why people quit their jobs is because of a bad manager.

In this chapter, we'll ask restorers directly: why do good people quit at your workplace? If you've read this far, the results will be hardly surprising, but they will highlight some serious blind spots in every restoration company, including yours. In an industry that largely promotes its leaders from within, there is a vicious cycle of mismanaged people carrying forward the torch of mismanagement. The industry needs nothing short of a management revival - will you be one of the first converts?

> The chasm between workers and managers is bigger than you think, and it's up to managers to fix it

Scan to tweet!

The Great Resignation could be a death blow to an industry already weary from employee retention issues. Or it could be a glass of cold water to the face, shocking managers out of their slumber and motivating them to give renewed energy and attention to putting the needs of the worker first.

> 66
> **People leave because of the toxic work environment and the favoritism.**
>
> - Gen Z Technician, Oklahoma
> 99

The answer lies in how seriously leaders take the complaints voiced in this chapter, and whether they're willing to humble themselves and admit that they, like many managers in the industry, are not even remotely on the same page as their workers.

The verdict is in, and it's the leaders that need to change.

Why Do Good People Quit?

Everybody has their own hypothesis on why good people quit their companies. Management has likely held countless meetings debating how they can keep employees longer, and the employees themselves talk about what went wrong whenever a talented colleague jumps ship. The problem in this case is that when there is such a massive divergence of opinions between two groups of people, finding a middle ground is rarely achieved without a big stick or a big carrot.

In theme with the rest of the Restoration Workforce Survey, we gave the microphone to hundreds of workers, asking them why talented team members chose to quit at the company they work at. As a manager, knowing your staff's collective response to this important question is critical for two strategic reasons. Firstly, when talented people quit, their colleagues pay careful attention, and secondly, because the answer your staff provide is likely the reason *they're* considering quitting as well, and speaking on behalf of a teammate that recently flew the coop is a great way to voice their concern with a glaring issue. Take note, as

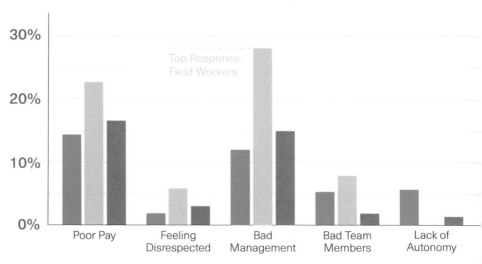

Why Do Good People Leave Your Company?

Responses from the 2022 Restoration Workforce Survey

their indirect feedback may be the root of something rotten that you need to address immediately.

The responses from workers, specifically field technicians, was not surprising.

The number one reason good people quit in their company, according to them, is because of management's incompetence.

Quoting one millennial technician, "Upper management is the absolute worst. They are very knee-jerk reaction based, and don't think about the repercussions of their actions as it relates to technicians. They don't train us well and give us too many hours with no work-life balance." Other field techs mentioned a toxic workplace, favoritism, and general lack of direction among their leaders that led to colleagues heading for pastures they believed to be greener.

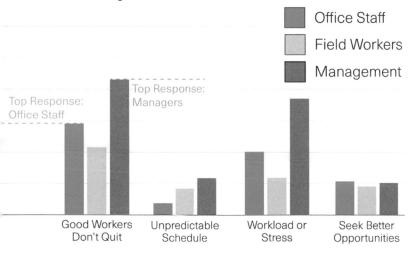

> ❝
> **Good people quit because they can't handle the amount of work and dedication it takes to be successful.**
>
> - Millennial Project Manager, Georgia ❞

The shocking revelation was how wildly this perspective contrasted with management's response to the very same question.

The clear, resounding theme when managers were asked why good people quit their company was that the premise of the question was flawed: good people don't quit.

Good people don't quit.

If someone quit, it means they weren't good to begin with.

This might seem like we're cherry-picking responses, but more than any other category, managers who responded to the Restoration Workforce Survey told us that if good workers left, it was because they simply couldn't handle the heat of the industry, and lacked the personal discipline required to be successful in restoration.

> ❝
> **They quit because of a lack of discipline. They can't even complete simple tasks and communicate poorly.**
>
> - Gen X Project Manager, ❞
>   Oklahoma

"Good employees leave because of a lack of will" one said, "a lack of ownership" cited another manager. Lack of organization, lack of discipline, a lack of work ethic, and lack of commitment all came up as well. Seriously, the word "lack"

Percentage of Workers Who Describe Their Relationship with Their Manager as Great

Responses from the 2022 Restoration Workforce Survey

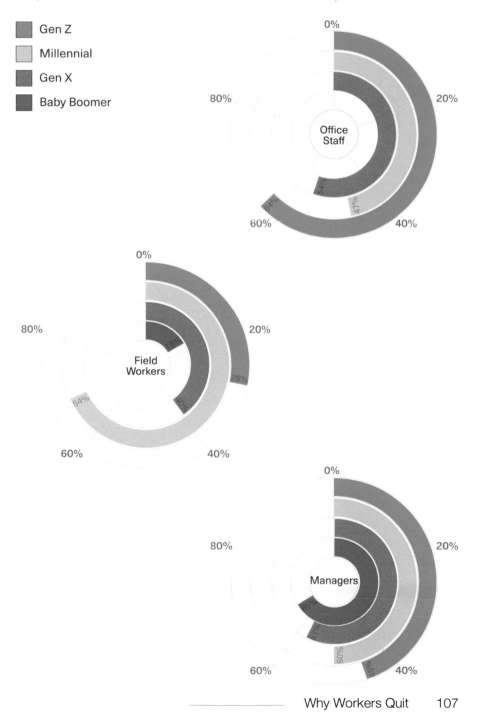

> ❝
> **The last 2 people that quit our company left because they didn't get along with the Project Manager.**
>
> - Gen Z Technician, Oklahoma ❞

appeared more than any other word among managers' responses to the question "Why do good people quit your organization?"

As in, it's the employee's fault they left. Not ours.

You don't have to be a psychologist or an evolutionary biologist to see the error in this antiquated 'only the strongest survive' mindset. The litmus test is simple - will the modern labor worker put up with this? The data says 'no'.

> ❝
> **No one leaves unless they don't want to be here anymore.**
>
> - Millennial Estimator, California ❞

The restoration industry is heading towards a giant iceberg if workers are increasingly leaving their jobs because of management's incompetence, and management's response is "Good! We didn't want you here anyway!"

This is an appalling disconnect between management and workers, and The Great Resignation has proven it's the workers who hold the cards.

We realized it was crucial to explore in greater depth the fraught relationship between management and employees. If there's any hope for improving things and creating an environment in the restoration industry where workers feel listened to, respect-

Managers and workers can't seem to agree why workers quit their jobs in the restoration industry, but it's the workers who hold the cards.

ed, and fulfilled, it would start with knowing where managers are currently falling short.

What Needs to Improve With Your Manager

We asked workers to describe their relationship with their direct supervisor or manager, and the responses ranged from "feels like family" (which we assume is a good thing, though not in all families!) to "sketchy", "fake", and "terrible". By and large, workers were satisfied with their manager, but there were large swings based on the worker's age and role.

> 66
>
> **My manager can come on a little strong. He often says things in a rude manner even though he doesn't intend to; it's something he needs to work on.**
>
> - Gen Z Technician, Oklahoma   99

Importantly, the Restoration Workforce Survey showed that field workers are generally much less satisfied with management than the rest of their colleagues, with Gen Z employees being particularly displeased with how they interact with their direct superiors. Again, if you're a manager reading this, the easy response is "well, that's a problem with this upcoming generation." Somebody is going to find a way to harness the energy of this upcoming generation to grow their business and make an impact in the lives of customers, and with such a mentality, you're guaranteeing it won't be you. If that's the case, you've already stamped your business with a time of death, and now are just waiting for the inevitable.

> 66
>
> **My manager needs to communicate better with us. Secret meetings and closed doors are not conducive to a productive environment.**
>
> - Gen X Salesperson, Rhode Island 99

Restoration workers are telling managers what they expect from their workplaces, but the majority of managers are not listening.

If you're interested in modifying your approach to improve your management's relationship with today's workforce, there's good news. They told us exactly what they're looking for.

Many leaders might look at the chart on the next page and breathe a sigh of relief that the most common response to the question "What would you change about your manager's approach?" is "nothing". Let us remind you that 36% of your workers approving of your management style is far from a ringing endorsement.

Instead, workers congregated around a few specific, tangible improvements that need to be made if their relationship with management is going to be salvaged.

> 66
>
> **Please, someone just get rid of my manager. She is ruining the company.**
>
> - Gen Z Technician, Idaho
> 99

First, as discussed in previous chapters, communication has to be way more intentional in the restoration industry than it currently is. As one worker put it, "I wish there were clearer goals and expectations in our company. Regular check-ins would help push me to continually improve in my role." Another worker asked for greater transparency, saying "We need more communication to our entire

> 66
>
> **Leadership just hired a new manager for my department who doesn't know anything about the industry. It's a slap in the face to us technicians who were told we'd have opportunities for upward mobility here.**
>
> - Gen Z Technician, Oklahoma
> 99

staff. Secret meetings and closed doors are not conducive to a productive work environment." Most staff show up eager to put their skills to work and move the ball forward, but getting tripped up because they don't know what they're supposed to be doing when, in what order, leads to wasted potential on a daily basis. Compound that wasted potential over weeks and months, and it's no wonder why workers begin to question if this company is the best fit for the time and energy they bring to the table.

Significantly, workers across the board also took issue with the temperament of their manager, describing personality short-comings that made it difficult to work for them, especially in an environment as stressful as restoration. In an industry where the assumption is that it's the field workers who are "a bit rough around the edges", it's surprising that so many workers point to character flaws their manager has that are starting to fracture their relationship.

What Would You Change About Your Manager's Approach?

Responses from the 2022 Restoration Workforce Survey

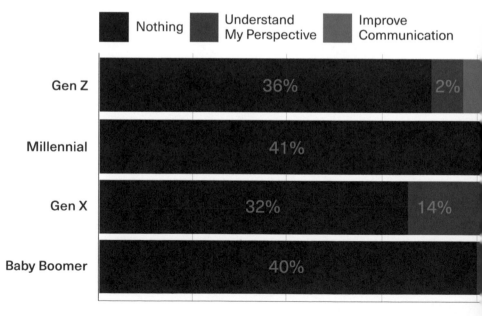

Examples of this include narcissism, a lack of patience, or a disrespectful way of interacting with other co-workers, and they all lead to the employee experience being worse than it needs to be. Today's worker cares just as much about where they're going as how they get there, and the best vision and mission statements in the world come crumbling down if they daily feel like they're being disrespected and belittled by their manager or supervisor.

Finally workers, especially millennial and older, felt like their manager didn't take time to understand their perspective, but instead would consistently bowl them over with directions or advice. As one worker put it, "I wish my manager would listen

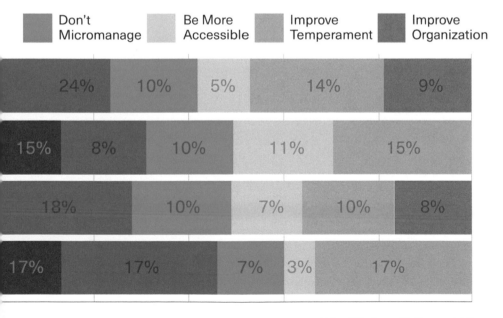

	Don't Micromanage	Be More Accessible	Improve Temperament	Improve Organization

24%	10%	5%	14%	9%
15%	8%	10%	11%	15%
18%	10%	7%	10%	8%
17%	17%	7%	3%	17%

more. Often it feels like he is more focused on what he is going to say next than who he is currently listening to." In a reactionary, fast-paced environment like restoration, slowing down and listening will not come naturally to most managers running on adrenaline. But as we've seen, workers want to feel like they are making a difference at work, and management showing they hear the workers' perspective and consider it can go a long way in demonstrating this.

Keeping Good Workers

If managers and leaders want to survive The Great Resignation, the way they relate to their workers must change.

We've seen a remarkable chasm between workers and managers in their perspective on why people leave their company. This has to change. If management believes talented workers are walking away from their company because of their own shortcomings, that needs to change.

> 66
>
> **My manager needs to shout less and be willing to listen to what those around him are saying.**
>
> - Gen Z Office Administrator, 99 Wisconsin

Any other response to the mass exodus of workers across the United States, and in the restoration industry, is utter foolishness.

The restoration industry has adapted to new technology and changing legislation. It has risen to meet the demand of increasing natural disasters, and even a global pandemic. Likewise, the future of the restoration industry is reliant on leaders to recognize the winds of change among today's workforce, and decide if those are going to be headwinds or tailwinds.

In the fast-paced, reactionary restoration industry, the managers that win with today's workforce are the ones that slow down to hear what they're saying.

Your management team will determine if you attract and retain the top talent necessary to grow and thrive amidst this new era of worker pushback, or if you will join the long list of companies whose old methods were no match for a new workforce.

If you're willing to humble yourself and check your biases at the door, we've got good news: there's a way out of this, and it starts with your managers.

> 66
>
> **My relationship with my manager is complicated. Some days we're on the same wavelength, and other days I'm tempted to quit because of their attitude.**
>
> - Gen Z Technician, Oklahoma
>
> 99

Model Candor & Assertive Communication with Your Management Team

It is astonishing how many managers were completely blind to the reality that many workers view management as the single biggest reason good employees quit. This reeks of an environment where leaders are being told what they want to hear, and are not being confronted with the brutal facts about their team's own flaws and failings.

It is imperative your company does not join the ranks of management teams that will walk blindfolded off a cliff because they didn't listen to the people saying "watch out!"

Make it a practice to say the whole truth to each other in leadership meetings, not biting your tongue because it may ruffle some feathers. Regularly analyzing internal threats and weaknesses, or asking the question "What are we missing here?" can force deep introspection as a management team and lead to confronting some brutal but necessary truths. If employees view leaders in your company as arrogant or disrespectful, they likely will not say it to your face. You need to create a culture where managers can identify these problems and address them without being worried about the interpersonal repercussions of doing so.

Managers in the restoration industry need to constantly be asking themselves, "What are we not seeing here?"

Scan to tweet!

This does not mean giving your leadership team license to be jerks to each other. This means making it clear to your top-level staff that more important than any one person's feelings is the shared responsibility you all have of creating a workplace that respects everybody and thrives amidst a changing workforce. Every person has their own unique set of blind spots, and healthy workplaces have a culture that identifies those blind spots, not to put someone down, but to manage and mitigate them. If employees can recognize that a manager on your team is a narcissist, one of his fellow managers should be able to recognize that too. If he hasn't been told yet that he speaks disrespectfully to staff, that is a management problem, not an employee problem.

Model Humility and Listening by Seeking Worker Input

Over and over again, workers expressed frustration when their managers talked, but didn't listen. Today's worker wants to feel bought in to where the company is going, like they play a key role in how your business will achieve its mission.

This will require your management and leadership team to show humility, acknowledge that you don't have all the answers, and instead intentionally solicit

> 66
>
> **I wish my manager would slow down, and ease up on micromanaging us.**
>
> - Millennial Project Manager, Ontario 99

feedback from your employees. When staff feel like they help shape the direction of the company, their loyalty increases and they are more likely to show ownership when new problems arise and new staff join the team.

In management meetings, ask supervisors how their direct reports are doing by name, and don't accept "good" as an answer.

> 66
>
> **My manager needs to improve her confidence. She is new to management and it's obvious she second guesses herself. If she is not confident in what she's telling us to do, it's harder to understand the reasoning behind what she's saying.**
>
> - Millennial Project Manager, Maryland 99

Take the time to find out what is working for staff and what isn't working. During weekly check-in meetings, encourage supervisors to ask their staff some of the following questions:

- What aspect of your job did you most enjoy this week?
- What work are you most proud of this week? What could have been better?
- Are there any barriers in your way right now?
- How can I support you better this upcoming week?
- How do you feel going into next week? Exhausted? Excited? Why?

Your only hope of bridging the growing divide between management and workers is to talk to them and truly listen to what they're saying. Workers were candid in the Restoration Workforce Survey about the problems they see with their company and their management team, and they would be candid with you too if you provided the opportunity for them to share their thoughts in a safe environment.

There is a massive chasm between today's worker and their managers, and those that can't bridge the gap will not survive.

> 66
>
> **When my manager is stressed, he needs to take some time for himself to sort through things before he approaches others and stresses them out as well. He'll be impatient, aggressive, or begin to micromanage others when he's experiencing work or personal stress.**
>
> - Millennial Manager, Washington 99

Invest Heavy Into Your Management Team

To accomplish all this however, you're going to need to step up the professional development for your management team big time.

Our survey showed evidence of managers across the restoration industry who had likely 'leveled-up' from field technician status without ever being trained on the soft skills required to manage and lead effectively. As a result, workers told us stories of being shouted at by managers, feeling manipulated and belittled, and like they weren't trusted to do their jobs well. Other survey responses indicated that managers needed improvements in their confidence, respect for other staff members, and ability to set standards and then hold people to them. As one worker put it, "I wish my manager was harder on slackers and could hold people accountable - it's letting the whole team down".

> 66
>
> **I feel like I'm walking on eggshells around my manager.**
>
> - Gen Z Technician, 99
>   Idaho

It's your responsibility to create a plan to help your managers overcome these soft skill deficits. Taking a talented operator and moving them into a management position might feel like a natural progression, but the skills that helped a worker exceed out in the field are different from the skills required to build a culture of trust and buy-in as a manager. As discussed in Chapter 3, your best bet is to detail the hard and soft skills required for a manager to succeed in your organization, and then create a training roadmap to address those who need improvements to meet your standard.

This is also a great opportunity for you to model listening and soliciting feedback. Ask your managers where they feel they bring the most value to the company, and what areas they would like to improve. Doing so will help them own responsibility for their professional development, and allow you to begin to build a culture where all staff value growth and improvement - an important aspect of attracting new workers and building a management team that accepts and acts on feedback.

> You cultivate what you honor. Recognize managers in your organization that are upholding your values.

Scan to tweet!

Confucius said that you cultivate what you honor. If you want to be a company that treats staff respectfully and models improvement, then uphold this to the rest of your team. Recognize managers who are working on their soft skills, and "call out" examples of your leadership team creating buy-in among their direct reports. Culture change won't happen overnight, but ignoring the growing divide between workers and their managers is a surefire way to wake up one day asking where all your good staff went. Consider yourself at a crossroads: you can either continue doing what you've done for years and hope that it will all work out in the end, or you can radically transform the relationship between your management team and your staff one supervisor at a time.

Yeah, But What About Money?

We can't ignore the fact that there is a percentage of workers who said good people quit a restoration company because they felt they were underpaid. When places like Target, Kroger, and Chipotle are offering $15/hour plus great benefits, there's the risk of a "race to the bottom" for employers, offering hand-over-first pay bumps at the expense of their margin just to retain staff.

What can restoration companies do in light of this? As Phillip Rosebrook, Partner at Business Mentors told us, "you need to link your paycheck with a purpose. Would a worker rather stand at a counter and make burritos all day long? Or restore lives and livelihoods after fires, floods, and other disasters?" If you can tell a compelling story of purpose, and link it to a real career path, you'll find employees who quickly realize that there's more to work than just the number on their pay stub.

>
> **People quit when they feel overworked and under-paid.**
>
> - Millennial Project Manager, Nova Scotia

This, again, will require you to listen. Find out what it is that your staff value most. "None of us have ever met someone who thinks they're overpaid, but we all know someone who we thought was overpaid," says Steve Cadigan, author of *Workquake.* This is proof that when employees start talking about how well they're compensated, what they really mean is "I

> **Our last employee left because they were offered better pay elsewhere. Personally, I would leave if the company didn't try and honor their word of promoting within the company.**
>
> - Millennial Project Manager, Maryland

don't believe what I'm giving is being matched by what I'm getting out of working here". The key then, according to Steve, is to listen to what's behind those statements of perceived value and fairness. "In this evolving market of compensation, companies must talk to their employees and discover non-monetary things their workers value that may cost little. It doesn't require a big budget, but it requires attention, a lot of listening and communicating, and being willing to break some rules along the way."

In this unprecedented era of worker pushback, it's up to leadership to create an environment that respects and honors workers instead of pushing them away.

Demonstrate humility. Model a desire to improve and grow. Don't ignore problems, deal with them head on. Assume every worker, whether they've been with your organization for 2 weeks or 20 years, could improve your organization in some way. If workers feel like they're undercompensated, find out what they're really looking for.

The fate of your business depends on it.

⋮☰ Key Takeaways: Chapter 6

⊘ Field workers believe the primary reason people quit is because of bad management. Many managers don't believe good people quit their company at all.

⊘ Field workers are far less likely to say they have a great relationship with their manager compared to office staff

⊘ Only 32% of staff don't have suggestions for how to improve their manager's approach. Others asked managers to listen better, improve their temperament, and communicate more effectively.

⊘ Companies that want to win with today's workforce need to overhaul their approach to management by modeling candor, listening to employees, and investing in training their leaders.

7

The Road Ahead

CHAPTER 7

Conclusion

The Road Ahead

J ohn D. Rockefeller said, "If you want to succeed you should strike out on new paths, rather than travel the worn paths of accepted success." It's time for you to completely re-envision how you approach today's worker, and we've got the data to prove it. With unprecedented access to restoration industry frontline workers, the Restoration Workforce Survey has proven that the old way of hiring, onboarding, and working with talent won't cut it anymore.

Today's worker demands their voices be heard, their mission be clear, their skills be developed and their workplace be enjoyable.

It sounds like a high bar, but it's well within reach for restoration companies serious about growing and strengthening their company amidst The Great Resignation.

Can your company offer these things? Because if it can't, another company will. You do not have the luxury of hoping this era of worker pushback is just a phase that will eventually regress back

Where Do You See Yourself in One Year's Time?

Responses from the 2022 Restoration Workforce Survey

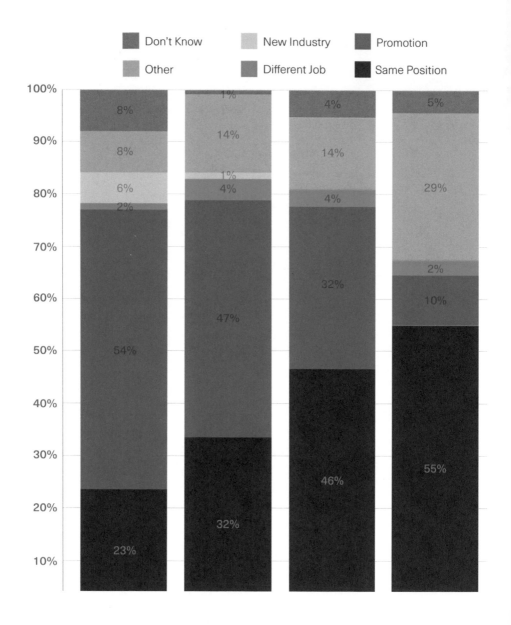

to normal. While headlines about The Great Resignation may come and go, the data tells us workers are expecting more of their employers, not less, and have no reservations about switching jobs until they find one that meets their needs.

Don't be one of the hundreds of restoration leaders that say "This is how the restoration industry is and always will be - workers just need to get on board." This industry isn't static. It's dynamic, and it can be improved. Change is not always fun, but it *is* constant. Bend, or break.

You must establish a positive team culture.

You must establish a consistent structure of company values and processes.

You must establish a more efficient way to train your employees. You have options; you don't have to take every single piece of advice in this book, but if you put this book down and your business looks the same as when you picked it up, you've missed the point.

Looking to the Future

Workers are telling us that they want to stick around in the restoration industry, if their managers are willing to improve their experience. Now that you have the data findings from the Restoration Workforce Survey in front of you, does your company have what it takes to still be around in five years? You've read the insights from restoration workers, you know what they expect. Can you deliver? Are you willing to try? There is no excuse for dying in the shrinking labor pool. The workers are out there, searching for fulfillment.

The restoration industry has a long, healthy life ahead of it if it's willing to give workers the voice they're demanding. You have the opportunity to lead and model the way - what you do with that opportunity is up to you.

A

Building a Better Workplace
for Women

Women in Restoration

Building a Better Workplace for Women

T he restoration industry has primarily been a male dominated workforce for decades. As a result, many of the decisions about what's working in restoration, what's not,
and where the industry should go, are made by men.

The Restoration Workforce Survey, however, was designed to
give a microphone to those whose voices too often go unheard,
and the women we surveyed provided some fascinating insights.

What blind spots does the industry have in its treatment of wom-
en that aren't being identified? What are the reasons women
have been left out of the conversation (and the workforce in
general) for so long? Are there any signs that things might be
changing?

The Restoration Workforce Survey provided answers to all of
these. In short, the future is bright, and there is a huge opportunity available to companies willing to make the changes necessary to take advantage of an increasing interest in restoration
among women.

In this appendix to *Why Workers Quit*, we will unpack what the Restoration Workforce Survey data says about how the experience of women in the restoration industry, the reasons why companies who are intentional in providing a better workplace for women have an inherent advantage, and the tangible steps you can take to become one of those companies, if you're not already.

First though, it's important to know where women are working in the restoration industry, and where they're not.

Participation in the Restoration Workforce Survey

Grouped by age and gender

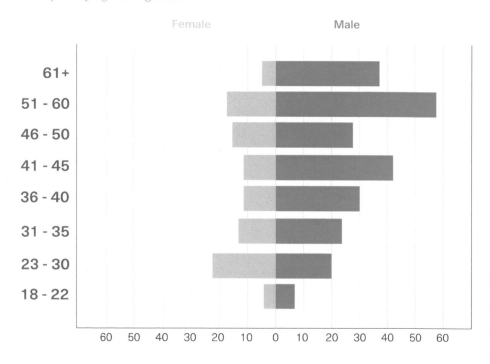

What the Data Says

Taking a look back at the spread of age and gender among Restoration Workforce Survey respondents, it's unsurprising that male Baby Boomers outnumber female Baby Boomers in the restoration industry by a significant margin. Frankly, you probably didn't need a survey to tell you that, as one look around your office would likely have confirmed this.

This largely holds true for Gen X employees as well, with a much larger portion of men than women working in the restoration industry among that age group.

> 66
>
> **We encourage women to move into leadership roles**
>
> - Gen Z Office Administrator, 99
>   Indiana

However, those advocating for better female representation in restoration should take note of the encouraging evidence that emerges the younger the workforce gets. While Millennial workers still skew male, there is far less of a gender imbalance than among previous generations. By the time we get to Gen Z employees, we see an almost equal gender balance between men and women in the restoration industry.

> 66
>
> **This is an area we're lacking. Other offices have a great working relationship and mutual respect for female employees, but there is a power struggle in our office due to a woman being in a leadership position.**
>
> - Millennial Office Administrator, Wisconsin
>
> 99

This is tremendous progress. An industry that has been dominated by men for decades is seeing increasing interest among young women workers - no small feat.

Breaking down industry tenure by gender only confirms this trend. Whereas men are distributed fairly in how long they've been working in restoration, over 70% of women have been in the industry less than three years. In fact, in the past year, just under 50% of people entering the restoration workforce are women. Businesses looking for new, undiscovered pools of workers would be wise to consider how they can better target and appeal to women considering looking for work in an exciting, fast paced industry.

There's the lingering question though, what role are these women taking? Traditionally in the restoration industry, men have gravitated towards the frontline worker jobs, whereas women have been more prominent in office support roles. Is this still the case today?

Restoration Industry Tenure, by Gender

Responses to the 2022 Restoration Workforce Survey

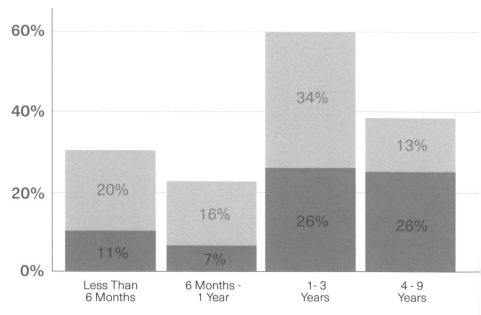

On the next page are two charts showing the breakdown of each role grouped by gender. The top chart shows where men and women above the age of 30 have gravitated in the restoration industry. Confirming many suspicions, the roles of Technician and Subcontractor are 95% male, whereas Office Administrator, Accountant, and Human Resources roles are strongly, if not entirely female. Additionally, leadership and management roles are strongly skewed male.

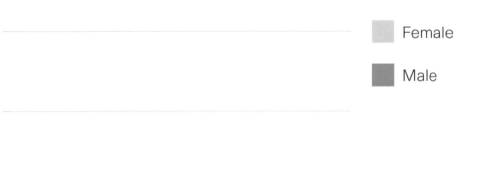

Over 70% of women in restoration have been in the industry for less than three years.

Scan to tweet!

However, below it is a breakdown of the same roles for workers under 30, and you'll immediately notice some differences. Most notably, the trend for Subcontractors and Technicians to be 95% male is being shifted significantly, with over 30% of young Technicians being female. Similarly, we saw a higher ratio of female Project Managers and Managers under 30 than their older counterparts.

The data is still coming in, so it's too early to conclusively say the restoration industry is

Female

Male

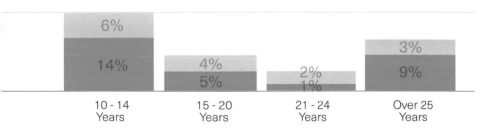

10 - 14 Years	15 - 20 Years	21 - 24 Years	Over 25 Years
6%			3%
14%	4%	2%	9%
	5%	1%	

Current Role of Restoration Workers Over 30

Responses from the 2022 Restoration Workforce Survey

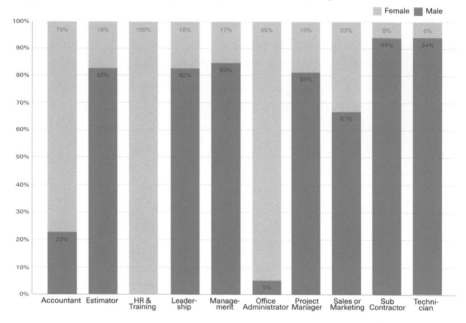

Current Role of Restoration Workers Under 30

Responses from the 2022 Restoration Workforce Survey

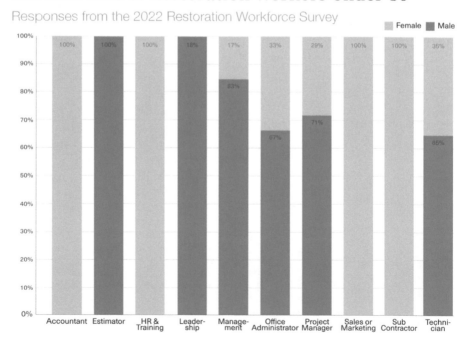

being rebalanced, but these are encouraging signs nonetheless. There are many factors that contribute to women or men believing that certain roles are not for them, but one of the biggest factors is not seeing themselves represented in the jobs they'd like to occupy. Seeing more consistent gender-balance across different roles can create a positive feedback loop, further encouraging people to pursue whichever job they'd like, as they see examples of others who look like them in similar roles.

Of course, equally important is understanding how these people are treated once they're in this role. Here's what survey responses told us about what it's like to be a woman in the restoration industry:

How to Make the Restoration Industry Great for Women

We asked survey respondents what their company did to make it a great place for women to work. Most importantly, the vast majority of responses among females said they felt their company was a great place to work already, and that they didn't expect or receive any special treatment. In fact, some women took issue even with the nature of the question, and didn't like the implication that special accommodations or consideration should be made for them.

For other women, it was clear that some intentionality on the part of their company went a long way to make them feel welcome

> 66
> **Our former General Manager started as an assistant, so her leadership and coaching is an asset to the women in our company.**
>
> - Millennial Office Administrator, Georgia 99

and able to juggle the various different roles they played in their lives. Companies that had policies that allowed for Paid Time Off when children were sick, or flexibility when appointments and family matters arose made women feel like their employer had their back. Other responses mentioned they were glad to see their company acknowledging that being a woman in a male-dominated industry can have its drawbacks. Many of these companies set up "Women in Restoration" groups or lunches, and had an open door policy when it came to discussing any issues or frustrations that came up.

And finally, maybe most obviously, equal pay, and heavy representation of women in all roles, made women feel more comfortable working in the restoration industry. Knowing that their office was 40-50% female told them that they would not be treated differently or alienated at their company, but instead would be able to work effectively alongside men, and each other, to accomplish the tasks set out in front of them.

Complaints about how they were treated were few and far between, but are still worth mentioning. One respondent described hostility between male and female workers, and feeling like she got walked all over in a male-dominated industry. Another woman described sometimes feeling excluded from team events and social interactions.

Importantly, some male respondents also described feeling alienated in roles that were largely female, and some male tech-

> 66
>
> **We are treated as equals. I do not feel any different for being a woman. We have more women in the field at this company vs my previous employer.**
>
> - Gen X Estimator, Ohio
> 99

nicians pointed to a divide between female office staff and male technicians that led to conflict at times. If the restoration industry is going to become a place that is equally welcoming to women and men, it will require more attention and focus, especially at the worker-level, to overcome the tendency to gravitate towards people that look and think like us, at the expense of others.

Why Strive for Greater Numbers of Women in Restoration?

It's worth begging the question, in light of all this, why strive to seek better representation among women in the restoration industry? The theme of this book has been "problems can be fixed, but it requires intentionality." Considering how much effort it will take to bring greater gender equality to the various roles within restoration, is it worth the effort?

If you're reading this book because you are having difficulty attracting and retaining talented workers, then the answer should be abundantly clear.

> 66
> **My company is flexible when I need time off for family matters.**
>
> - Gen X Office Administrator, 99 Washington

Women make up 51.1% of the population in the United States, yet only 29% of the restoration industry overall is female. Among critical, valuable roles such as Technicians and Managers, this percentage is far lower.

We know it's not due to a lack of interest, as young women are increasingly pursuing these careers, even if they've been historically dominated by men. Instead, it's due in some part to hiring managers mistakenly believing the next generation of workers looks similar to previous generations.

Restoration companies looking for talented pools of available workers should begin to think about what they can do to better appeal to women considering the trades. Combined with structured, comprehensive onboarding described in Chapters 2 and 3, businesses could recruit women that other companies may be overlooking, train them in all the company's processes and procedures, and give them a rewarding career.

Additionally, having more women on your team, in various roles, provides advantages beyond just increasing the quantity of workers available. "Women, in general, are very nurturing and intuitive," says Julie Johnson, Owner of Alpha Omega Disaster Restoration. "They have a keen sense of how to come alongside people going through a difficult situation. Women on my team have walked through the valley of extreme stress with our customers; hugging them when they cry, taking the time to listen when they need an ear to hear, making dinner for them when they see they can't muster one more thing, the list goes on."

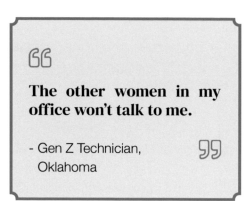

> 66
>
> **The other women in my office won't talk to me.**
>
> - Gen Z Technician,
>   Oklahoma
>
> 99

Restoration companies should be quick to recognize the advantages that women can bring to certain roles. For example, many female customers may prefer to have a female technician working in their home, alongside their male co-workers. There are also benefits of having women Project Managers, working with customers through the highs and lows of seeing their home restored. As Shelli Bagwell, Lead Estimator at Belfor Property Restoration described, "If there is an irate customer, women are good at de-escalation and finding a solution. The restoration company that recognizes the differences in the way women work will benefit from enhanced customer service, credibility among industry professionals and community organizations, and a balancing perspective for any business needs."

Tangible Steps You Can Take

The verdict is in. There is a tremendous opportunity available to companies who can recognize that the restoration workforce is shifting more female, and are willing to make the changes necessary to provide a workplace where women are welcomed and thrive.

For those eager to take advantage of the opportunity in front of them, here are a few tangible steps you can take to build an environment that's more welcoming to women.

Identify Your Values

As we've mentioned elsewhere in the book, everything comes down to what your company values. Many leaders fail to clearly and consistently articulate their company norms and values, and in such a vacuum, employees will substitute their own. According to Ashlee Hofberger, Vice President of First Onsite Property Restoration, the first step in creating a culture that welcomes women is identifying those high-level company values. "First, you define what your cultural norms are; what is acceptable and

> 66
>
> **I was the first female area manager at the company I work for. Before that, I held roles as a Coordinator, in HR, and as IT. They let me try new things and if I set my goals towards something they moved mountains to help me achieve it. They regularly built me up and invested in helping me grow as a team member.**
>
> - Millennial Manager, Pennsylvania
>
> 99

what is not." With this front of mind, it's easier for employees to identify behavior exhibited by staff, or company policies, that don't align with these values. "We encourage our team members to ask 'How does this align with our core values?'" Ashlee told us. "I've been in several meetings where this one question redirected the whole conversation." Likewise, if workers have habits (intentional or unintentional) that create an unwelcome environment for certain individuals, grounding feedback in your company values gives you the ability to point to an objective, shared standard that all employees are held to.

Develop Your Staff

Too many companies rely on traditional stereotypes and assign roles based on gender as opposed to leaning in and understanding the unique strengths of each individual. "If an all-male team or office gets a female employee," says Shelli Bagwell, "there is a tendency to let administrative and housekeeping tasks get pushed on the female, all under the expectation that they are naturally better at those things." This delineation of labor typecasts workers and sends the signal that women wouldn't be able to help their company address a shortage of Technicians or Managers. Instead, welcoming environments look at the strengths and weaknesses of each individual, and create personalized development plans just for them.

"Put people in places where their strengths are used for the greater good," advises Shelli. "Identify paths for advancement and plans for professional growth - for both men and women."

> 66
>
> **We are treated as equals. I do not feel any different for being a woman. We have more women in the field at this company vs my previous employer.**
>
> - Gen X Estimator, Ohio
>
> 99

Over time, your company will see more male office administrators, and more women in field roles, if that's where their skill sets align. You'll be able to harness the unique talents each worker has for the greatest impact, as opposed to artificially limiting your workforce's productivity based on preconceived gender roles.

Think About The Big and Small Stuff

There are hundreds of interactions, big and small, that women have with your company, their co-workers, and with customers that send the signal that they're either welcome, or they're not. As a leader, you need to think about the message being sent by both the big things (your values, your policies, your processes and structure) and the small things (your office space, your uniforms, your communication) in your business. Many female workers were particularly thankful for company flexibility surrounding paid time off, acknowledging that sometimes sick kids or doctor's appointments can interfere with the business of the day. Additionally, creating avenues where employees felt comfortable talking to their supervisors if they didn't feel they were treated respectfully went a long way in showing that women had support from managers and leaders in their organization.

> **My company is flexible when I need time off for family matters.**
>
> - Gen X Office Administrator, Washington

On the simpler side, employers must also think about the message being sent through the microinteractions women have with their workspace and other co-workers. "Not to be funny or diminish the issue," says Shelli, "but little things like making sure the shared restrooms are kept clean and that the cleaning is not defaulted to the women is a way to incorporate a co-ed team fairly. Another simple thing that can be done is ensure you have uniforms made for women. So many uniform standards are uncomfortable and unflattering to females. Acknowledging those differences while maintaining consistency can be difficult, but should always be top of mind when hiring women for a uniformed position."

Restoration companies that will succeed among today's worker are the ones that recognize that employees, both men and women, want workplaces that treat everyone with respect. Companies that get this right have the opportunity to capitalize on growing interest among women in restoration, and find new pools of workers they never knew existed. Though the industry is seeing some positive trends incorporating women into roles they've traditionally been excluded from, it will require intentionality from employers to carry the torch the rest of the way. Those willing to take up this mantle will be the ones that have the most to gain.

66

My company has hired a lot of women, including in positions of management.

- Millennial Accountant, Maryland

99

Will you be one of them?

Want an exclusive presention of the most relevant insights from this book for your management team?

Limited spots are available for an exclusive training session featuring the most valuable insights from the Restoration Workforce Survey, and the impact it will have on your company's ability to attract and retain top talent.

Scan this QR Code for more info!

Harnessing the Power of a
Multi-Generational Workforce

Different Age, Same Mission

Harnessing the Power of a Multi-Generational Workforce

The results from the Restoration Workforce Survey should have a massive impact on how employers relate to their workforce. For the first time, leaders and managers have clear, tangible data on what workers do want, and what workers don't want; why they join your company, and why they quit.

The most fascinating aspect of all this was the nuance that was contained within all the answers. As interesting as it would be to say, "All workers care more about finding fulfillment than they care about salary", the truth is murkier. *Many* workers care about finding fulfillment in their work, but certainly not all. As we sliced and diced the data, we realized that workers' preferences tended to group together based on their role (whether they're in the office, in the field, or management) and their age.

This is important because it has a direct impact on how effectively you can apply the lessons from this book. The better you know the specific motivations, however divergent, of each individual worker, the better you can build a workplace that appeals to all of them.

If you can build a company that takes advantage of the energy and enthusiasm of young workers alongside the wisdom and experience of more tenured staff, you'll be able to take advantage of the unique skill sets each of them bring to your company.

The goal of this short appendix is to help you do just that. In it, we'll unpack the areas where we saw the most divergence between different age groups, dive into the implications of it, and the ways you can harness the power of a multi-generational workforce in your restoration company.

Restoration companies that succeed in this new era are not ones that forgo hiring young people because they are too complicated, nor do they completely do away with the "old guard". Instead, they recognize that each worker has unique interests, strengths, and motivations, and when working together, they build a restoration company that is better than the sum of its parts. If you already have a multi-generational workforce, then the ingredients are all right in front of you. Let's get started.

What the Data Says

What roles do Gen Z workers gravitate towards? How about Millennials, Gen Xers, or Baby Boomers?

Many people might think that young workers start out in the field, and then slowly migrate towards the office before eventually landing in management at the end of their career. According to the data, these people would be wrong.

> 66
>
> **My first few weeks on the job felt harder because of my age.**
>
> - Gen X Technician, Michigan
>
> 99

While there are slight trends in this direction, there is a consistent age spread across roles. For example, while 16% of management are Baby Boomers, so are 11% of field workers. Likewise, you'll find sizable portions of Millennials and Gen Xers across every role in your organization.

This means that assuming your next field worker will be young, or that a good manager will have decades of experience, is limiting your talent pool. Likewise, you'll have to consider different

What is Your Current Role? Grouped by Age

Responses from the 2022 Restoration Workforce Survey

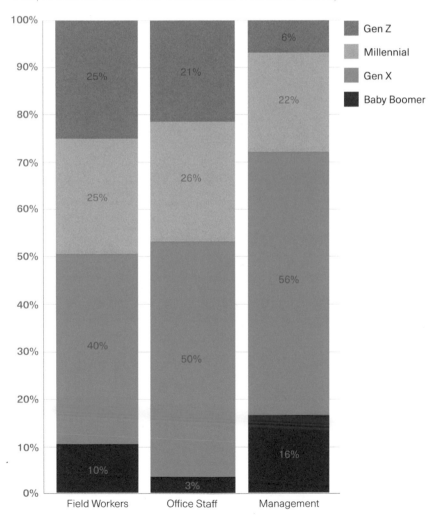

What are the Reasons You Accepted Your Current Role?

Responses from the 2022 Restoration Workforce Survey - Grouped by Age

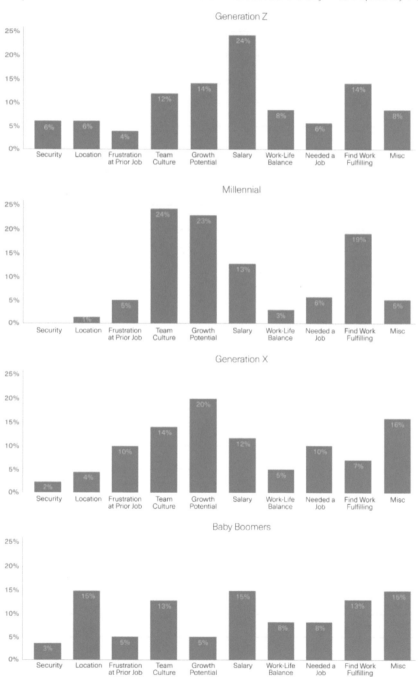

age dynamics as you develop your organizational structure, roll out new software, plan workplace events, and more.

Would a young manager be comfortable leading a field worker twice their age? How would their direct reports handle this age dynamic? This would likely require intentionality and coaching from your leaders, to help the young manager learn how to overcome any perceived barriers because of their age difference. Likewise, if your field workers are planning a team culture event, even if that's just grabbing a beer at the end of a hard work day, it's important to be conscious of the different stages of life your workers may be at. Older workers may have family responsibilities that impede them from participating in evening or weekend events, but it's still vital they be included in team culture activities that build trust and rapport among your frontline staff.

> 66
>
> **I accepted this position because I was looking for better pay with health benefits.**
>
> - Baby Boomer Office
>   Administrator, Idaho 99

Different age groups also have different motivations for joining your workplace. We looked at this data in Chapter 2, but wise managers are cognizant of the different factors that influence why an employee joins their organization, and they leverage these to help retain and get full productivity out of their staff.

> 66
>
> **I love the core group of employees we have here. It feels like everone is a family.**
>
> - Baby Boomer Office Administrator, Montana 99

For example, the primary reasons Millennials and Gen Xers join a company is because they are attracted to its team culture and are looking to grow their career. If your company can promise either of these factors, you'll have a good chance at being able to recruit workers in this age group. Workers in this age group are far less concerned about job security, work-life balance, and even salary, and are willing to sacrifice these to work at a company that is investing in their personal growth and surrounding them with colleagues they enjoy working alongside.

Contrast these motivations with the youngest generation entering the workforce: Gen Z employees. These workers care moderately about team culture and growth potential, but their chief concern is salary. As mentioned earlier, this age group's exposure to global recessions, pandemics, and more has led them to prioritize job security and knowledge that their job will help them make ends meet in an unpredictable world.

Baby Boomers have similar motivations, but for different reasons. Nearing the tail end of their career, they are less influenced by growth opportunities or moving up the corporate ladder. Instead, they want a decent salary, good work-life balance, a location that is convenient for them to get to each day, and a bit of job security.

Knowledge of why each different age group chooses your company over a competitor can help you tailor your pitch during the hiring process and customize a worker's role to capitalize

> 66
> **In one year I'd like to be in the Owner-CEO role. Three years from now I'm hoping to be retired.**
>
> - Gen X Estimator, Ohio   99

> 66
>
> **I hope I'm still working this time next year, but with the world like it is right now, and because of my age, I'm not sure if that will be happening.**
>
> - Baby Boomer Office Administrator, British Columbia 99

on what they're looking for. Maybe you take a percentage of the resources you've allocated for a Millennial worker's salary, and put it towards professional development instead. Or you could intentionally create a role for Baby Boomers that has less on-call work, but also less opportunity to be paid overtime.

Similarly, when we asked workers where they saw themselves in one year's time, it's hardly surprising that the answer "retirement" appeared more often among Baby Boomers than it did among Gen Z workers (included in the 'Other' column on the next page).

Early on in their career, Gen Z and Millennial employees are still trying to determine if restoration is the right industry for them, and whether the role they've taken within the industry is a good fit. They want the flexibility to be able to try different job functions, and possibly move into management. Many young workers told us in one year's time they saw themselves growing in responsibility, or moving from the office into the field, or vice versa.

Into the latter half of their career, these workers are less interested in upward mobility or experiencing different job functions within the restoration industry. Instead, responses to the Restoration Workforce Survey tells us they are more interested in improving their expertise within the role they're in, planning for retirement, or opening up their own business.

Where Do You See Yourself in One Year's Time?

Responses from the 2022 Restoration Workforce Survey

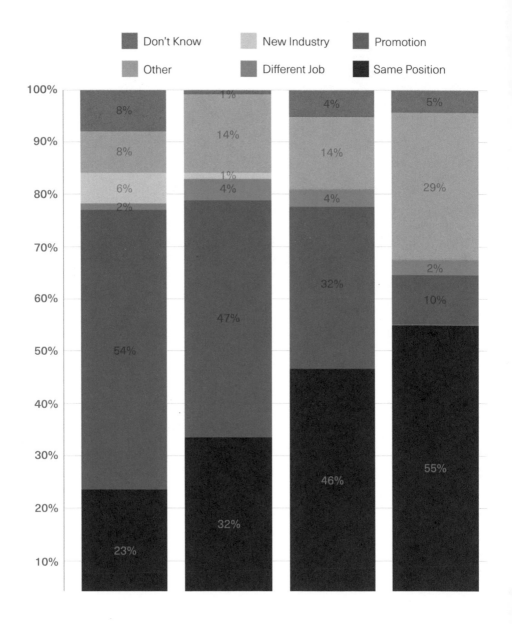

> ## 66
> **In one year I hope to be working only 3-4 days a week. Three years from now, I want to be down to 2-3 days.**
>
> - Baby Boomer Managerr, Pennsylvania   99

Understanding these different dynamics are critical for employers that want to build richly rewarding experiences for their employees, regardless of their age or personal goals. Your workers bring different skills to the table, and they want to get different things out of working with your company. Your success as a multi-generational employer depends on your ability to weave these different perspectives together and take advantage of your diverse workforce.

Harnessing The Power of a Multi-Generational Workforce

Too many restoration owners today focus on creating uniformity, where every worker, regardless of their age, gender, or background, is expected to look, think, and act the same. It's easiest to just create a single mold that every worker should fit into, but leading a business this way significantly limits the potential horsepower you can get from your team.

> ## 66
> **I love the team culture here. The owner invests in our personal and professional growth.**
>
> - Gen X Supervisor, Idaho   99

In the same way the human body has different parts with different functions (eyes see, ears hear, feet run), restoration companies that want to succeed with today's workforce recognize the specialized skills and expertise each individual brings to the team.

This means asking the question, what do the Baby Boomers on my team bring to the table, and what can they teach my younger workers? Likewise, how can the Millennials and Gen Xers on my team take their enthusiasm for team culture and professional development and use it to improve the work experience for my entire company?

For Chuck Violand, Principal of Violand Management Associates, this looks like finding opportunities for your seasoned workers to display how your company values and norms influence day-to-day operations at your company. "Beginning with the company's core values," Chuck says, "your tenured employees can lead by example while purposefully highlighting and explaining which core values they are displaying each day in their decisions and their actions." For new, young employees, their first interaction with your company values will likely be during the hiring process or their onboarding. It's up to your leaders and older staff to show that these are not just words on a page, but your values influence everything your team does, from how you intake a new job to how you estimate a loss or correspond with insurance.

Likewise, you can harness the experience of your tenured staff members to document your company know-how into, well, KnowHow. Many of these workers have learned the hard way how to correctly complete a Cat 3 water loss, for example, and

> 66
>
> **I've observed that young people will leave our company because they want to try a new career. Older workers will quit because they are physically getting worn out and don't want to do on-call shifts anymore.**
>
> - Millennial Manager, Washington
>
> 99

you can wield this battle-tested knowledge to benefit not just them but your whole company by documenting their expertise and making it accessible to all workers.

Many restoration businesses unwisely have the success of their company wrapped up in the brains of a few seasoned knowledge keepers. As discussed in Chapter 3, this creates a situation where hard-fought lessons don't get passed down to new workers, except via the convoluted telephone game. Honor your experienced workers by giving them the opportunity to codify their knowledge and expertise into your company process hub, ensuring what they've learned lives on past their time with the company.

> **I love being encouraged to learn new skills and apply them to growing the company.**
>
> - Gen Z Salesperson, Utah

Similarly, younger workers are passionate about creating healthy team cultures that make everyone feel included, and are likely to seek a direct connection between the work they're doing and the impact it makes in the life of a customer. As a leader, you can empower these workers to lead the charge in capturing customer stories, sharing them with the rest of the team, and thinking about how your workplace dynamics can be improved. The energy and enthusiasm young employees can bring to some of these important company issues will improve the experience for all staff, regardless of age.

Working Together to Build a Better Restoration Industry

While managers can take advantage of workers' differing motivations for working in the restoration industry, it's also critically important for them to highlight and double down on what their workforce has in common.

They show up every day to help restore homes and lives. They're united by your company banner and uniform, and have committed to pursue your company values. With a shared vision and mission, they can wield their unique skills to play a tangible, sizable role in making a difference in the lives of your customers.

What's required is humility. The ability to acknowledge that though everyone has a different perspective and different motivations, those that are willing to learn from one another and adapt we can build a restoration company that takes advantage of differences that span age, gender, and role.

As Steve Cadigan, author of **Workquake** puts it, college basketball is a great example of this. "15 years ago, Coach Mike Krzyzewski of Duke University was furious about the new generation of star basketball players joining his team. Most only wanted to play for Duke for one year instead of the typical four before turning pro, so Coach K swore he would never recruit kids that weren't 'loyal' to the team.

"Unfortunately, Duke began losing - a lot. They lost to teams they would never lose to. This prompted Coach K to begin thinking about the problem differently. He reframed his dilemma by saying 'building a new team every single year is going to be challenging, but if I am going to win the NCAA championship I have no choice but to adjust.' As a result, he changed his approach and embraced the challenge of incorporating a new generation of players into his team."

> 66
>
> **We've got an amazing culture here. Everybody really has each other's best interests at heart.**
>
> - Millennial Manager, Washington   99

If you know much about college basketball, the rest is history. Coach K built a dominant basketball team that was, at one point, the best team in the country. He recognized the unique skills that his players had, but also the change in approach he would require in order to harness those skills.

Restoration leaders have a similar opportunity. You've got a diverse team at your disposal with different motivations for joining your squad. You can either dig your heels in, wishing everybody saw things the same way you see them, or you can adapt and recognize the opportunity that's available if you can harness the focus of a diverse workforce towards a singular goal. Whether it's a vibrant team culture, fulfilling work, job security or upward mobility, your team is looking for you to provide different things. In the same way, they have different skills and expertise they can bring to the table. Unleashing their full potential may require humility and adapability, but doing so can lead your team and your business to both personal and business success.

> **I like that we get to work with a diverse group of employees and customers.**
>
> - Baby Boomer Manager, Maryland

Acknowledgements

This book was a big undertaking, so we have lots of people to thank. First we need to recognize the contributions of the whole team at KnowHow. Everybody, whether they directly contributed to this book or not, played a big role in ensuring we could deliver on a project this massive while still simulatenously continuing to provide unparalled service to customers and evolving and improving our software every week.

We also want to thank all our industry partners (see full list on the next page) who helped us shape the questions for the survey, collect responses, and analyze the results. The Restoration Workforce Survey was a collective effort, and we benefitted from having some of the best minds in the industry come together for the purpose of improving and advancing the whole industry.

Thanks to Michelle Blevins at C&R Magazine for all the work she did in helping get the word out about the Survey and the book, as well as Valerie King at R&R Magazine and Eric and Larry of Morning Tech Meeting from Blue Collar Nation.

Thanks to Andy Earle, Steve Cadigan, Chuck Violand, Tim Hull, Phillip Rosebrook, Julie Johnson, Ashlee Hofberger, and Shelli Bagwell for the expertise and perspective they shared throughout the course of this book.

Finally, most importantly, thanks to the hundreds and hundreds of workers in the restoration industry who completed the Restoration Workforce Survey. Your insight, openness, and candor gave us the opportunity shine a spotlight on the best and worst parts about working in restoration, and how the industry can make the changes necessary to thrive for the next decade.

We're very optimistic about the future of the restoration industry, and are excited to play a big role in making it better for workers everywhere.

Restoration Workforce Survey
Industry Partners

BUSINESSMENTORS

GEARHART & ASSOCIATES, LLC.

RESTORATION TECHNICAL
INSTITUTE

Looking to further improve your restoration business?

Download KnowHow's e-book

"Delivering 5-Star Restoration Experiences: An Analysis of 1,000 Bad Online Reviews in the Restoration Industry"

at

fivestarrestorer.com

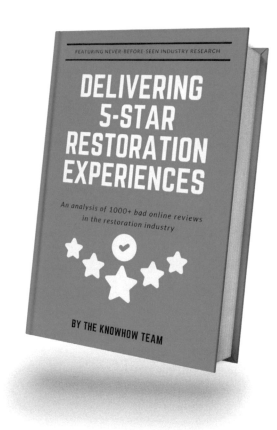

CHAPTER 2

POOR COMMUNICATION & WORKMANSHIP

THE MOST COMMON PROBLEMS IN THE RESTORATION INDUSTRY (ACCORDING TO CUSTOMERS)

If you had to wager a guess, where would you expect most restoration jobs to break down? Delays? Rogue technicians delivering bad customer service? Negative experiences with insurance?

According to the multitudes of upset customers on Google Reviews we uncovered in our analysis, there were two primary issues that stood out far above the rest.

In fact, 57% of all the complaints we analyzed fell into two categories: poor-quality workmanship provided by technicians, or poor communication between the business and the customer. This will come as no surprise to anyone who has spent time in the industry, but these issues are pervasive and have an outsized influence on whether a project was deemed a success or a failure; a 5-star project, or 1-star disaster. We'll tackle both of them in-depth, starting with the number one contributor to a bad online review in the restoration industry:

The Price of Poor Communication

According to our analysis, the biggest issue that plagues restoration companies today is a breakdown in communication. Anyone who's ever been in a relationship for more than an hour knows that communication problems are inevitable, but the impact of poor communication on a restoration job can be particularly consequential. Narrowing in on the issues cited in our analysis, the vast majority of these complaints stemmed from one of three situations:

- Employees agreeing to meet customers at certain times and then not showing up.
- Major communication breakdowns between the restoration and rebuild teams upon hand-off.
- Management or customer service "disappearing" when a customer had complaints or questions about their bill.

For most of the examples cited in this section, the formula was the same: the restoration business would make a commitment, and then when plans changed, or when more information was needed, they would become unreachable. Countless tales were told of customers taking time off work, or cancelling plans in order to meet an employee, only to be left hanging without warning or any explanation. Oftentimes, multiple calls placed by the customer to reschedule were not returned, or worstofall, rebooked only to once again have the employee not show up. For customers who experienced these "no-shows" from the busi-

> **66 I have called them for service no less than 5 times to no avail. The three times they made an appointment with me they were 4 or more hours late and did not even bother to call me.**
>
> ———— Clearwater, FL

ness, this perceived disrespect by the restoration company was compounded by lost income or vacation time that often accompanied the customer's decision to take the day off work to meet the contractor. In some situations, the review was written in real time while the customer was waiting for the contractor to show up or answer the phone, leading them to take their frustration directly to Google Reviews.

Shockingly, there was one communication issue that was so common, we had to create our own category for it: customers never being contacted after asking for a quote. Story after story was told of a customer on a tight timeline (e.g., house currently flooding), reaching out to request an estimate or assessment, only to be left hanging. Unreturned voicemails, promises to send someone out left unmet – a startling 9.4% of all 1-star reviews we analyzed cited businesses failing to follow up with their customers. Talk about losing the game before it even starts – for companies who received reviews like this, potential customers had already negatively impacted their Google Review rating without ever having had the chance to meet them. Their inability to return a phone call or follow through on a commitment lost them business both in the moment, and potentially in the future as well.

> "
> **Once our kitchen was gutted for mold treatment our house sat for weeks with no activity. Our contact was not reliable, he would push out dates and lie - I was in a hotel from August until December.**
>
> ———— Augusta, GA

There are many reasons stories like this could emerge, from a lack of clear expectations set, to the business not being adequately prepared to handle capacity. Yet, considering how sim-

> **“ It took this company five months to do an 80-Sq.
> Ft vinyl floor replacement and flood repair. I
> literally called them weekly for 2 months before
> it got done. Very slow service, but of course their
> billing is prompt and they're happy to threaten
> me with legal action on Christmas Eve.**
>
> ———— North Salt Lake, UT

ple it is to pick up the phone, it's a shame that so many businesses lose customers like this unnecessarily. Especially when we know how bad reviews can negatively impact future revenue, who knew that not following up with a prospective client could hurt you, both in the moment (lost revenue) and in the future (a bad online review repelling future customers). However, of all the communication issues we came across, these may be the least destructive in nature.

REGARDLESS OF WHO WAS AT FAULT, IT'S THE RESTORATION COMPANY THAT BEARS THE BRUNT OF A CUSTOMER'S ANGER Our analysis was filled with horror stories of customers complaining about selecting a restoration company for a job, having their home quickly gutted, only to be handed off to a renovation team and receive radio silence indefinitely on how the rebuild was going. Customers described living in hotels for months on end, while struggling to maintain contact with the business in charge of reconstruction of their home. Unreturned phone calls or being passed around from employee to employee without any straight answers plagued these customers, who just wanted life to return back to normal. In many cases, usually out of sheer exasperation, the customer would finally just pay out of pocket to bring in a new company to finish the job.

It's important to note that in situations like these, even if the fault and communication breakdown was the result of a third party company in charge of the rebuild, it was the **original restoration company** who bore the brunt of the customer's anger and ultimately the negative Google review. A job well done on the restoration side was not enough to leave a customer satisfied, and communication issues from a separate party often tarnished the entire experience for customers. This means that simply "handing off" a project once your work is complete is not enough. If your business is the first point of contact for the customer, it means they will hold you responsible for the end result, regardless of whose fault a lacklustre final product is.

One of the actions that created some of the highest level of frustration from customers (though unsurprising) is how quickly communication issues vanished entirely once it came time to collect payment for a job. Companies that were difficult to get ahold of during the restoration and construction phase suddenly were very eager to know the status of their payment. In some situations, customers told stories of jobs not even being completed and they were threatened with legal action or liens if they didn't pay up. After being evasive about timelines or progress for weeks or months prior to distributing an invoice, this double standard left customers upset, frustrated, and turning to Google Reviews to make their voices heard, warning others to avoid a fate similar to theirs.

1-Star Workmanship

The other beast that consistently reared its ugly head throughout our analysis (29.9% of the time to be precise), were customers complaining about poor-quality workmanship during the restoration or rebuild phases. In addition to turning to Google Reviews to warn others, customers would turn to insurance providers for rectification, which often forced companies to come back and re-do work, sometimes two or three times, before work was done to a standard every party was satisfied with. These are truly lose-lose scenarios, as it left customers frustrated, obliterated margin for the restoration company, and frustrated insurance adjusters as well (potentially impacting future referrals).

By the time the customer was posting their opinion on Google, the 1-star review was a long time coming, guaranteeing that the poorly executed job would continue to haunt the restoration company into the future.

Not included in this category are projects planned poorly, leading to delays, or negative interactions between customers and technicians – this meansthat almost 30% of all 1-star reviews simply boil down to a customer being left with a product that missed their expectations entirely.

Complaints in this category usually centered around one of three main issues:
- A final product that began to deteriorate in only a few weeks or months
- Jobs left incomplete
- General negligence on behalf of the contractor

Most common among these were staff cutting corners during the repair and rebuild process, either out of laziness or not know-

> 66
>
> **They replaced the flooring 2.5 years ago. Six months after the install, I contacted them to let them know the flooring was separating. They took months to respond, and after a series of e-mails and unreturned phone calls the 2-year warranty expired. I now have to fix the flooring at my own expense. Poor workmanship, do not trust this company.**
>
> ———— Fort Wayne, ID

ing the right way to do things. In many situations, contractors performed a sub-standard job, which very quickly led to cracks, chips, bubbling, or further repairs that needed to be completed (at the cost of the restorer). Instead of taking action to mitigate a potential molehill before it turned into a mountain, many customers reported restoration companies avoiding the issue, blame-shifting, or completely going silent.

> **They used sub-contractors on my job and they did poor work; did not complete and had to be called back; never cleaned up daily. Contractor stapled down a sub-floor with no glue. All the staples came up through the tile flooring and I had to tear it all out and do it again.**
>
> ———— Louisville, KY

Once again, in many situations it was the second half of the project where things broke down. Customers described demolition and mitigation going according to plan, only for sub-contractors whose role was to come in and "do the easy stuff" to do a poor job, leaving a place much worse than it was originally. Shoddy work, safety violations, and a rushed work job forced customers to reach out to insurance to bring things back to working condition, frustrating both them and the company and damaging the company's reputation with referral partners in the process.

EACH WORKFLOW AND TASK MUST BE CLEARLY DEFINED AND ASSIGNED

Frequently, businesses would tackle everything but the last 10% of a job. Customers told stories of businesses "wrapping up" prematurely, leaving them with holes in their walls, exposed wiring, or dust and debris that they needed to clean up themselves. Some reviews complained about equipment being left at a customer's house indefinitely on a job half-done, while others described employees clearly skipping critical steps. This left additional work above and beyond the original scope, to be completed by either the business, or in some cases, embarrassingly, the customer to take on themselves.

As tempting as it might be to cut corners (or allow corner cutting) in the moment, we've all been around long enough to know that, it eventually comes back to bite us. Usually, this will take the form of negative Google Reviews, decreased margins, and a damaged reputation among customers and insurance adjusters. However, in some situations, the cost of negligence or laziness can be far worse. Sadly, a few reviews mentioned remarkably dangerous mistakes from restoration companies that could have ended in death, including gas leaks and carbon monoxide exposure due to inattentiveness from workers. Let these stories serve as a wake-up call on why communication and quality issues are not to be ignored.

> **They put indoor closet doors on exterior storage room doors. The doors are falling apart now after just a few years!**
>
> —————— Charlotte, NC

Lessons for a 5-Star Restorer

Thankfully, when looking at the list of communication and quality issues that make up almost 60% of the complaints on 1-Star Google Reviews, there's one clear takeaway: none of these business problems are unsolvable.

If your restoration company is anything like those mentioned in these reviews, you can begin to make a tangible impact on customer satisfaction by taking some relatively easy steps. For example, you can reset expectations within your company by announcing concerted future efforts to return phone calls and send emails you've committed to send. If the problem of "communication falling between the cracks" plagues your organization, it likely rears its head in other areas too. Instead of viewing it as an indictment, view it as found money: low-hanging fruit (e.g., returning a phone call) that could begin to drastically impact your business' professionalism and customer satisfaction.

Of course, one reason communication problems spring up is because when things aren't going well, it's human nature to avoid uncomfortable conversations (e.g., communicating a project delay). Fortunately, in our analysis, many customers were sympathetic to plans changing on the fly, or projects taking longer than expected, especially if it was the result of something outside the company's control (e.g., a natural disaster). However, no shows or delays without any explanation, left customers feeling disrespected and angry, and used up any patience they might have been willing to extend to the business. Your employees likely do not love writing long essays, but teaching your staff to "just hop on the phone" when they need to give customers an update, will pay dividends in the long run. It takes a while to change the habits of your team, but implementing the practice of taking an extra few minutes to reach out to customers ahead of time will save your team headaches in the long run, and preserve the reputation of your business.

TEACHING YOUR STAFF TO 'HOP ON THE PHONE' WILL PAY DIVIDENDS IN THE LONG RUN

Poor-quality workmanship is a more difficult problem to weed out, but is still possible to address, as long as the root causes are understood.

As the President of the Restoration Industry Association, Mark Springer knows the importance of ensuring that across the United States, restoration businesses are keeping their promises and performing high-quality workmanship. From his perspective, maintaining consistency comes down to two factors: "First, the workflow for each type of service must be mapped with each task and the person responsible for it clearly assigned," Mark said. "Understanding how the various business functions work together to create the end result of a satisfied customer is very important. Second, training for the execution of each step of the workflow must be prioritized with a goal of constant improvement."

In most cases, employees or contractors have the desire to deliver a high-quality final product, but lack the training or skill to deliver it consistently. With the wide variety of tasks restoration contractors are required to perform, from water mitigation to mold remediation, smoke damage to biohazard clean-up, it is understandable that there may be gaps in a worker's knowledge or skill set. The best restoration companies find ways to supplement their employees' expertise by standardizing their processes and internal know-how and making those available to all team members. This ensures office staff or frontline workers don't miss any steps, ensuring no customer falls through the cracks and no critical task is skipped out in the field.

MAP OUT THE WORKFLOW FOR EACH TASK, AND DEFINE THE PERSON RESPONSIBLE

In some situations, certain team members will have low ownership over the success of the business, and as a result will be inclined to skip steps or make careless mistakes. These people, in the roles they're currently in, are toxic to your organization. Their apathy may be the result of finding the work unfulfilling, a skill gap that can be easily overcome, or bigger character problems that need to be addressed. Assertive, mature discussions with these individuals are the only way to remedy this,but be warned – putting this off will not resolve the problem on its own, and will likely only make things worse.

The responsibility to address these problems starts with management. According to Chuck Violand, Principal at Violand Management Associates and leader in the restoration industry, the key is to define your expectations, and then do the hard work of holding tension to those expectations. "The best way to maintain accountability to a high-quality final product" says Chuck, "whether that product is a project, the financial performance of your company, or simply a tough conversation, is to clearly articulate what the final product should be, and then maintain the discipline to hold your team and the organization accountable to consistently deliver it. Accountability always flows from the top, and many business owners struggle with that."

Turning the ship around if you are plagued with bad reviews due to poor quality workmanship or communication issues requires intentionality and discipline, but neither are unavailable to anybody in your organization. Combine a crystal clear focus on improving communication and worker competency with the right tools and buy-in from your team members, and you'll be able to make a tangible indent into the issues that are keeping your team from providing the type of experience customers are expecting and hoping for.

Download the full e-book for free at

fivestarrestorer.com

Eliminate Inconsistency

With KnowHow, workers do things the right way, giving your managers their time back and freeing you up to grow rapidly

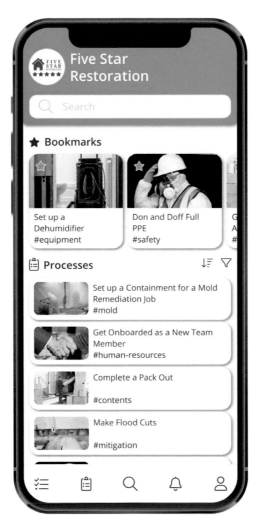

Request a demo at **tryknowhow.com**

Want an exclusive presention of the most relevant insights from this book for your management team?

Limited spots are available for an exclusive training session featuring the most
valuable insights from the Restoration
Workforce Survey, and the impact it will
have on your company's ability to attract
and retain top talent.

Scan this QR Code for more info!